Taking Down the Defenses

Taking Down the Defenses

A Collection of
One Hundred Brief Essays
and Meditations

Arthur Foote

First published in 1972 for Unity Church, Saint Paul,
Minnesota, by Essex Publishing Company, Essex
Junction, Vermont

First published as a Beacon Paperback in 1977
by arrangement with the author

Published simultaneously in Canada by
Fitzhenry & Whiteside, Toronto

Printed in the United States of America

(paperback) 9 8 7 6 5 4 3 2

Library of Congress Cataloging in Publication Data

Foote, Arthur, 1911-
    Taking down the defenses.
    Reprint of the ed. published by Essex Pub. Co., Essex
Junction, Vt.
    1. Meditations.   I. Title.
[BV4832.2.F62   1976]   242   76-7743
ISBN 0-8070-1117-7 (pbk.)

UNITY UNITARIAN CHURCH
732 Holly Avenue, St. Paul, MN 55102

*To the "family of families" that is Unity Church of Saint Paul,
in grateful remembrance and abiding affection*

Taking Down the Defenses

1 TAKING DOWN THE DEFENSES

"There appears to be a conscience in mankind which severely punishes the man who does not somehow and at some time, at whatever cost to his pride, cease to defend and assert himself, and instead confess himself fallible and human."

— CARL GUSTAV JUNG (1875-1961)

The theme that runs through many of the brief essays and meditations of this book might be called "Personal Disarmament." Every person needs to stop defending himself — defending himself to others, but first of all to himself. Until he does successfully put aside his pretences and self-assertions, as Jung insisted, "an impenetrable wall shuts him out from the living experience of feeling himself a man among men."

Psychoanalysis is one way, a long and costly way of taking down that "impenetrable wall," rock by rock. The Roman Catholic confessional has sometimes provided another way. A third route is the ancient practice, known in every major religious faith, of setting aside time for daily, private devotional use; a regular period for quiet thinking, for personal examination, for reestablishing one's own priorities, for gaining an honest image of oneself.

Our age suffers more from loss of solitude than from evaporation of belief. Beliefs are important; truthseekers do not take them lightly. But loss of solitude, of a private devotional life, jeopardizes the whole quality of one's life. Socrates long ago affirmed that "the unexamined life is not worth living." A healthy self-examination can bring our lives under thoughtful scrutiny, judgment and evaluation. It is often said that how we act is more important than what we believe. Very likely so. Then let us stress the importance of one kind of action — the act of going apart; of cultivating the art of "quiet sitting," as the Chinese Sage called it, of deliberately turning one's back on family and friends, daily responsibilities and all distractions, to engage in what may variously be called "prayer," "contemplation," "meditation," or simply straightforward reflection upon life and our relation to it.

Granted it is a difficult habit to establish. We lead busy, active lives. We are always running out of time. We find it extremely easy to rationalize that this old-fashioned practice isn't really as important as the business deadline we have to meet, the shopping

1

that needs to be done, and the chores we've already put off too many times. But the truth is that just as nations find it hard to get down to brass tacks on military disarmament, so do individuals find it difficult to cease defending themselves and to get on with the sometimes painful and always demanding task of personal disarmament.

First of all, we must convince ourselves that taking down the defenses is as important to us individually as disarmament is to mankind collectively. Consider these words of the late Judge Learned Hand:

"You may build your Towers of Babel to the clouds; you may contrive ingeniously to circumvent Nature by devices beyond even the understanding of all but a handful; you may provide endless distractions to escape the tedium of your barren lives; you may rummage the whole planet for your ease and comfort. It shall avail you nothing; the more you struggle, the more deeply you will be enmeshed. Not until you have the courage to meet yourselves face to face; to take true account of what you find; to respect the sum of that account for itself and not for what it may bring you; deeply to believe that each of you is a holy vessel unique and irreplaceable; only then will you have taken the first steps along the path of wisdom."

This book is designed to help us meet ourselves face to face, and to take true account of what we find. Its one hundred passages have not been written for casual perusal, for amusement or relaxation, nor for rapid reading in search of information. Rather are they meant for pondering; like the starter in a car, to start your mind turning over. And like your car, sometimes the mind starts almost instantaneously, sometimes only after much cranking and several false starts. Once the motor does start, you disengage the starter. These meditations are to be used similarly. Remember that reading can be an escape from solitude, an avoidance of thought. Use it as a prod, not a crutch. If the opening quotation suffices to get you "under way," put the book away. When you come to the end of a passage, don't read on. You have set this time aside for quiet renewal of imagination and resolve, to go to work on the life-long task of demolishing the defenses of your own creating that sever you from others and hide you even from yourself. No one else can take down those defenses for you.

"Maturity consists in no longer being taken in by yourself."
— AUTHOR UNKNOWN

"We do not have enough inwardness, we are not sufficiently preoccupied with our own spiritual life, we lack quietness; and this not only because in our exacting, busy existence it is difficult to obtain, but because, ignoring its importance, we do not take pains to secure it, being too easily contented with living our lives as unrecollected men who merely aim at being good."

— ALBERT SCHWEITZER (1875-1965)

Most of us live our lives almost exclusively in the active tense. We are "activists" — we think that to live is to make things happen, and tend to scorn the passive life of contemplation. To be preoccupied with one's spiritual life has come to be considered morbid, a symptom of illness. Our prescription for spiritual health has been to let the soul strictly alone. Keep busy and "on the move," keep your mind occupied — this has been the order of the day. But living is not only doing and acting; it is allowing life to flow in upon us. It is drawing aside, from time to time, to be an observer, a receiver.

There is morbid introspection, of course, but not all introspection is morbid. The good doctor of Lambaréné, looking at Western civilization from the perspective of his observation post, saw that we need to strike a better balance between the active and the passive tense. We need to study to be quiet, to consider better who we really are, and what are our true ends. This is not advocacy of monastic withdrawal, nor the world negation of some Eastern religions. Dr. Schweitzer found the superiority of Christianity in its vigorous affirmation of the world, in its wrestling with human suffering. But there must be times of withdrawal, of honest recognition of spiritual proverty, of firm resolve to secure a better balance between inwardness and outwardness, between being and doing. Otherwise we shall live "our lives as unrecollected men who merely aim at being good."

"We moderns are faced with the necessity of rediscovering the life of the spirit; we must experience it anew for ourselves. It is the only way in which we can break the spell that binds us to the cycle of biological events."

— CARL GUSTAV JUNG (1875-1961)

3

AN OPEN LIFE

"All deceit begins in self-deceit."

— THEOLOGICA GERMANICA (14th Century)

Perhaps the most pernicious kind of dishonesty is that which we perpetrate upon ourselves. Many who would not consciously lie to others do deceive themselves. We concoct excuses readily, and easily accept our "good" excuses as unadulterated truth. Inward truthfulness, as the ancient words above remind us, precedes outward honesty and openness. As we are with ourselves, so shall we be with others. No decent, self-respecting person can lie to others without first lying to himself.

Thomas Jefferson, writing to Peter Carr, gave a never-to-be-forgotten rule: "Whenever you are to do a thing, though it can never be known but to yourself, ask yourself how you would act were all the world looking at you, and act accordingly." Jefferson did not mean kowtowing to convention or weak conformity to the ways of the world. If we are really standing for the best in life, we shall often find ourselves — as has been said of Jesus — "maladjusted to the status quo." But the existence of a higher order of morality than the world demands, or even allows, does not mean we shall want the cloak of secrecy to protect us.

A major reason for the practice of a daily devotional discipline is to assist us toward what may be called "an open life." The man who withdraws to solitude for patient self-examination, who looks at his own life, his activities, his motivations, his achievements, his self-excusings as under the eye of God, does not fool himself so easily.

"Demeane thy selfe more warily in thy study than in the street. If thy publique actions have a hundred witnesses, thy private have a thousand. The multitude looks but upon thy actions: thy conscience looks into them."

— FRANCIS QUARLES (1592-1644)

4   WHAT WILL PEOPLE SAY?

"Only the way of wholeness and integrity
Can guard the soul.
Guard it so that nothing is lost,
And you will become one . . . . .
It is of this that a rustic saying speaks, which says:
The crowd cares for gain,
The honest man for fame,
The good man values success,
But the wise man, his soul."
— CHUANG TZU (Third and Fourth Centuries B.C.)
(tr. by Arthur Waley)

How often you hear it: "What will people say?" And what a poor excuse it is. But, being truthful with ourselves, how often we recognize it is this very thought that holds us back from doing something we otherwise would. The opinion of others is important to us, often to an unfortunate extent. We want to be well thought of, and do not think well enough of ourselves to forego frequent reinforcement in the form of the approval of our peers, our friends and neighbors. So we conform, in trifling or in stifling ways. We refrain from saying what we really think. We try, in ways we ought not to, to live up to the expectations of others. Instead of being just ourselves, with quiet if stubborn insistence, we bend to the pressures to do and be what others expect. Bit by bit we surrender a measure of our freedom, not wanting to be thought queer and off-beat.

Granted, being members of society and not hermits, there is a proper regard for what others think. Good manners lubricate human relations. Thoughtfulness and consideration are ways of caring for others. And a good deal of non-comformity looks suspiciously like what some psychologists call "attention-getting mechanisms." Nevertheless, when we ask, or privately think: "What will people say?" our concern is generally less than admirable. We are in the act of knuckling under, of allowing some little bit of our integrity to be washed away.

How well Emerson put it, in *Self-Reliance:* "What I must do is all that concerns me, not what the people think. This rule, equally arduous in actual and in intellectual life, may serve for the whole distinction between greatness and meanness. It is the harder because you will always find those who think they know what is your duty better than you know it. It is easy in the world to live after the world's opinion; it is easy in solitude to live after your own; but the great man is he who in the midst of the crowd keeps with perfect sweetness the independence of solitude."

It is clear that this gracious gentleman was not blind to man's need to cooperate, to be kind and considerate. Good citizenship must often involve compromise, the bowing to majority decision, the ability to be a good loser. But, he rightly insisted, "nothing is at last sacred but the integrity of your own mind." Because this is so, every man should resolutely guard that integrity. It is often not easy to know the point where it is threatened. Only if we are thoughtful, observant and honest with ourselves can we hope to know the line we must not cross.

"I will so trust that what is deep is holy, that I will do strongly before the sun and moon whatever inly rejoices me and the heart appoints."

— RALPH WALDO EMERSON (1803-82)

5   INTO THE SILENCE

"Be able to be alone. Lose not the advantage of solitude . . . but delight to be alone and single with Omnipresency . . . Life is a pure flame, and we live by an invisible sun within us."

— THOMAS BROWNE (1605-82)

If the seventeenth century needed such advice, how much more the twentieth. All the world is brought into our living room today. By radio, television and myriad other contraptions is our privacy invaded, our isolation destroyed. Beyond the ability to be alone, there is the problem of guarding at least a few moments each day for ourselves, with all "the world" shut out. Yet only through a carefully nurtured capacity for self-recollection can we learn who we are and what is our true vocation. We recall the passage in Amiel's *Journal,* where he counsels: "The man who has no refuge in himself, who lives, so to speak, in his front rooms, in the outer whirlwind of things and opinions, is not properly a personality at all. He is one of a crowd, a taxpayer, an elector, an anonymity, but not a man."

Most of us dread going "into the silence." We have lost the ability profitably to be alone — lost it through disuse, like the burrowing mole who has become blind. If we retire to be alone, it is no delight. Our minds do a hop, skip, and jump; we find ourselves unable to concentrate. The beds unmade, the letters unwritten set up a clamoring demand, and we experience none of the tranquility we have come apart to enjoy.

But this is only to say that the discipline of solitude is difficult, and our own disorganized condition pitiful. The only remedy is to learn this art anew. One can only learn to swim by swimming; one can only learn the "advantage of solitude" by faithful practice. And, like swimmers, we must learn to not thrash about, but entrust ourselves to the buoyancy of the silence. For silence has a real buoyancy; and the power to collect our thoughts by withdrawal from the outward to the inward is the way to discover that life indeed "is a pure flame" and that there is "an invisible sun within us" by which we truly live.

"Consider the significance of silence. It is boundless, never by meditating to be exhausted, unspeakably profitable to thee. Cease that chaotic hubbub, wherein thy soul runs to waste, to confused suicidal dislocation and stupor; out of silence comes thy strength."
— THOMAS CARLYLE (1795-1881)

6 THE HIGHEST GOOD

"Happiness is the best, noblest, and most pleasant thing in the world."
— ARISTOTLE (384-322 B.C.)

Aristotle, in his *Nicomachean Ethics,* called happiness the *summum bonum,* the highest good. To "pursue happiness" is one of man's inalienable rights, according to the Declaration of Independence. If so, man certainly needs a clearer understanding than he generally appears to have of what constitutes happiness. How often people say they are happy when they mean that they are contented, or are enjoying themselves. Contentment is a nice state of being; but the word is no synonym for happiness. A cow is contented if properly cared for, but we should hesitate to call her happy. Human beings, if fairly healthy emotionally, if not anxious, hungry or in pain, are reasonably content. A happy man may know a good deal of contentment; but he will also sometimes experience what is called "divine discontent." He will be disquieted by the wickedness of the world, the sufferings of the innocent, the sickness of society. There will be too much he wants to see changed to allow him undisturbed contentment. Still, in his discontentment with his present achievements, or the state of the world, he may still be happy.

Neither is happiness the same as joy. If contentment is a quiet, relatively passive state, joy is an active, bubbling, highly transient state. Joy is akin to ecstacy; too intense an emotion to be experienced often or long maintained. Happiness, on the contrary, is not explosive, nor momentary, nor nearly as unpredictable.

Pleasure, likewise, should not be confused with happiness, although most people avidly pursue it and tend to regard its pursuit as their inalienable right. Many things give us pleasure. Unfortunately, pleasures are not always harmless. One of the troubles with sin is that so many sins are highly pleasurable, at least for the moment. But Aristotle was quite right in insisting that happiness does not lie in pleasure, or amusement, or crowding as much fun as possible into one's days and years. Pleasant and innocent activities are all very well; they have their proper place in life. They are not, however, what constitutes happiness. In fact; happiness seems curiously independent of physical comfort, of pleasure-seeking and fun-loving. A multiplicity of possessions, a trouble-free life, a gourmet cuisine, a playboy existence are none of them roads to happiness.

What constitutes happiness, Aristotle insisted, is "virtuous activities." Thus he put his finger on the all-important distinction between fun, pleasure, and even joy and happiness. They are all possible without integrity, without guiding principles and high moral standards, but happiness is not. Happiness is a virtue, the fruit of right living. It is a state of being, not a transient feeling. It is the quality of a whole life, the result of thought-out values, high standards of personal rectitude, and worthwhile objectives that give life purpose. This highest good is ours to the degree that we ourselves are able to achieve a healthy relationship to life, and to death; to our fellowmen, and to ourselves.

So understood, happiness is our proper pursuit, our inalienable right.

"Man is the artificer of his own happiness."

— HENRY DAVID THOREAU (1817-62)

8

THE LOST ART OF DREAMING

"How shall Americans learn again the lost art of dreaming?"
— PHILLIP WYLIE (1902 -   )

One may question whether many Americans have ever really mastered the art; few besides the Quakers, at any rate. But the tempo of life increases, the rate of change accelerates; hours of solitude and quiet reflection become more difficult to come by. The need to learn this "lost art of dreaming" grows acute. Our lives are dangerously externalized. We prattle of "togetherness," but fail to find much of it. True community is only possible among persons who have learned to pay attention — to themselves, to their neighbors, to the world about them, and to what T.S. Eliot has called "the uninterrupted news that flows out of silence." How little genuine community we can discover in all our busyness. We are active, ambitious, and grow weary with doing; yet we accomplish disappointingly little really worth accomplishing. Our lives are cluttered with possessions, distracted by ambitions, passions, wants, and worries.

Being alone and being with others are too complementary to be regarded as opposites. We cannot really be with others if we are in fact running away from ourselves. We cannot be loving and happy persons unless our ability to affirm ourselves grows out of our solitude and privacy. And the opposite is just as true. Only by knowing true community, by being loved and affirmed, can we learn how to love others and to affirm ourselves. While we are with others, we must seek to establish genuine community by paying attention and really trying to understand. But we are not apt to be much good at this if we are not willing to frequently withdraw from society, in order to learn what the Hindu philosopher-statesman, Radhakrishnan, calls "the art of letting things grow in quietness."

Like all serious art, this is not learned in a few easy lessons. The artist knows he must practice faithfully, day by day, year after year, before mastery of his medium is his. So must it be with the serious student of the spiritual life. And what do we do, how do we practice? It looks deceptively like doing nothing. We sit quietly, alone with our thoughts, not thinking so much as simply holding a thought, some bit of wisdom — as one might hold a gem in one's hand, turning it over and around to see what it will reveal. We let life flow around us, through us, and try to become more fully aware of ourselves, of others, of the great mystery of existence. Where the "uninterrupted news that flows out of silence" comes from is not essential for us to know. It may come from the deeper levels of our own being. It may come from some "collective unconscious" such as Jung tried to chart. Or we may conclude that our minds are but the channels through which this "news" flows from some profound Source of Wisdom. But whatever the source, we are not to surrender that final responsibility which each of us owes to himself. These "messages" are not to be embraced uncritically. They could be only the sly prompting of the amoral "Id," which is quite capable of playing impish pranks. But they are to be "tuned in," weighed carefully, until we are convinced we have an authentic word of wisdom. And if not the "voice" of God, at least the voice of our own better nature.

The lost art of dreaming is nothing occult or mystical. Meditation is simply a kind of thinking — a kind not limited to brilliant minds. Brilliance may be more hindrance than help, in fact. We ought not to expect "a mystical experience," a sudden flash of illumination, such as we may have read about in the journals of the mystics and saints. Such things do occasionally happen, but they are difficult to evaluate. Most probably they will not happen to us. The test of meditation is not what we think happens, or fails to happen, in our solitude. It is whether through it we gradually become freer, wiser persons. Have we merely been led for the moment into some supposed "spiritual state," which vanishes when everyday life returns? Or have we been brought to stand more securely on reality, and thus more able to be true to ourselves and to others? Have we become calmer, steadier persons, or even more vacillating and tense, when the pressures are applied once more? Have we grown more able to give love, to respond to others in meaningful, helpful ways, or have we only become more hopelessly involved in ourselves?

Just to ask such questions is to know that the art of meditation is an arduous path that few indeed would ever attempt, were they not driven by awareness that life is "an engagement very difficult" and that to quit ourselves like men we must make a significant place for quiet contemplation.

"If your soul is a stranger to you, the whole world becomes foreign."
—KABIR (1440-1518)

10

OUR FIRST DUTY

"There is a luxury in self-dispraise;
An inward self-disparagement affords
To meditative spleen a grateful feast."
— WORDSWORTH (1770-1850)

The possession of a conscience is not an unmixed blessing. Pascal shrewdly observed: "Men never do evil so fully and so happily as when they do it for conscience's sake." Without a conscience, a man is certainly less than human. But history records many crucifixions, many stonings and burnings at the stake done by highly moral men acting in obedience to their conscience's counsel. We have come to speak of the puritanical conscience, harsh, demanding, unforgiving. We need to stress what Swami Vivekananda taught: "Our first duty is not to hate ourselves."

A puritanical conscience is not only apt to do damage to others; it is bound to be harmful to its owner. "How shall we expect charity towards others," asked Sir Thomas Browne, "when we are uncharitable to ourselves?" The malfunctioning conscience is, in fact, one that first destroys a man's self-esteem; it then allows him to project his own self-hate out into the world and onto other people. The conscience develops healthily in childhood when the family is a happy unit, the parents loving and understanding, clear and forthright in their ideals, and firm in their guidance. Where these ingredients are not in sufficient supply, conscience develops, but not entirely wholesomely. It tends to function in ways that are devious, harmful, and self-defeating. It becomes an obstacle to self-acceptance. By making unreasonable demands, it induces self-hate, a hatred often unrecognized, for our true feelings about ourselves usually come out disguised as our feelings about others.

Despite the ancient wisdom that urges us to love others *as we love ourselves,* few of us, it seems, fully realize that it is literally true; we cannot love others without also respecting and accepting ourselves. When we are filled with resentment towards others, the real source of the difficulty usually lies in our hidden resentment of ourselves. Our unwillingness or inability to forgive others stems from our inability to forgive ourselves.

This is the most difficult kind of forgiveness, this self-forgiveness. When conscience is overly harsh and punitive, we may appear to others as gracious and respectable, our overt behavior above reproach. Only the most perceptive will detect in our actions the confusion in our motivations. There is truth in the saying that it is possible to "kill with kindness." We do many apparently kind and generous things that hurt because they are done in subtly condescending ways. Behind the façade of virtue lie our own neurotic needs. There is, for instance, our insatiable hunger for the approval of others, since we really don't approve of ourselves. Or consider the seldom-recognized hostility we discharge upon others via the practical joke, or juicy bit of gossip. It is the unacknowledged condemnation of self that leads so many to become witch-hunters, and super-patriots, and to join organizations of the far right — for conscience's sake, of course.

Jesus laid great emphasis on God's forgiveness and shocked the Pharisees with his readiness to dispense it. Perhaps in freely offering divine pardon he may have erred on the side of mercy. Who knows how many whom he told "go thy way and sin no more" were able to follow his advice? But what Jesus did understand was man's need to feel forgiven. To his beatitudes let us add: "Blessed are they who heal us of self-despisings; for they make it possible for us to love our neighbors."

I am not advocating a lenient, complacent attitude toward our own shortcomings. Genuine repentance and such restitution as is possible must precede any forgiveness we are to grant ourselves. But what I do claim is that a tyrannical conscience is every bit as bad as a stuffy complacency. A man forever running himself down can never get up.

"Respect, for others and for oneself, is at the root of every virtue; disrespect, at the root of every vice. The respect and disrespect take many forms."

— AN HASIDIC SAYING

9 MEN NEED REMINDERS

"God must be brought to birth in the soul again and again."
— MEISTER ECKHART (1260-1327)

Men need reminders that they are called to more than animal and sensual life. We have rejected monastic asceticism, hair shirts, and the various other forms of mortification of the flesh. Still, these were ways of reminding men that the stubborn flesh needs mastering. "The angelus, matins, and vespers, and the wayside crosses help many to remember the Spirit within."

We need reminders, reminders that we are more than we are, that we carry latent capacities, the faint beginnings at least of spirituality. We can use whatever aids are available to help us recollect that we are called to a life above and beyond the life we are now living. The Sabbath is one such reminder. Even for the Sunday golfer, or for the lie-at-home-in-bed, the sound of church bells calling men to worship must stir some thought that we are called to be athletes of the spirit.

All of us deeply need, at least once a week, to recall ourselves to the higher purposes of our lives, the real ends of our existence. There is wisdom in planning one day a week as a day of re-creation. There is need for play, for relaxation, for a change of pace. There is also need to "let one's deleted surface consciousness lie fallow" in order "to give the deeper levels of the mind a chance to present their intuitive knowledge."

Dr. Oliver Wendell Holmes, asked why he went to church, replied that he had a plant called reverence which need watering each week. If we go, let it be for the same reason: to rededicate ourselves to our ideals, to restate our faith, reflect upon our aims and goals, and re-estimate our worth as bearers of something divine in our hearts.

One should not go to church unprepared for such serious endeavor. A bit of old-fashioned advice, then: along with putting on your Sunday best, prepare yourself psychologically, emotionally, spiritually. A little quiet time, a few moments with some favorite devotional classic, the silent repetition of a poem or psalm or hymn can be ways of getting ready. "Mankind became artists in ritual," wrote Alfred North Whitehead in *Religion in the Making*. "It was a tremendous discovery — how to excite emotions for their own sake, apart from some imperious biological necessity." So, clear the stage of the trivial, the unworthy, the anxious thought. Plan to keep the morning leisurely, if you can. Arrive at church early, your spirit expectant, your mood reverent. Remember Emerson: "I like the silent church before the service begins better than any preaching."

Here is time for quiet thinking, for recollection, for rededication. Thus prepared for, it is far more likely that the experience of church going will be a rewarding one, and an effective reminder of our true vocation.

10   THE WAY OF A SIMPLETON

"Everyone says that my way of life is the way of a simpleton. Being largely the way of a simpleton is what makes it worthwhile."

— LAOTSE (Sixth Century B.C.)
(tr. Witter Bynner)

As our Western world rushes madly along, not knowing where it is going, and seldom even stopping to ask, the wisdom of this old "Simpleton" of 2500 years ago becomes convincing to more and more of us.

"The way to do is to be," we read in Laotse's *Tao Teh Ching*. To our anxious question: Does life have any meaning? a simpleton replies: Does that question have any meaning? The meaning of life is found in the living of life. Life has meaning because we find it meaningful. The healthy-minded person is too fully engaged in living, too absorbed in satisfying his curiosity, testing his powers, to spend his time worrying if it is all worthwhile.

When asked by a Moslem disciple how he could experience Allah, the Sufi mystic simply slipped off his voluminous tunic and stepped out into the pouring rain. Lying on the grass he opened his mouth and spread his arms. When he returned to his questioner he said: "That's how." This is the way of a simpleton, content to speak in parables, knowing one cannot find God at the end of a syllogism. God is not a concept to be argued about, but an old name for a profound experience. Throw open the doors of your being, and there He is. Or it is. The Psalmist must have belonged to the wise fraternity of simpletons, too, when he wrote: "O taste and see that the Lord is good."

The simpleton is not callous, blithely unconcerned about the "giant agony of the world." The misery of the innocent moves him to compassionate action; the mess men are making of the world tempts him to despair. Confronting a Dachau, a Hiroshima, a Vietnam, he probably feels as keenly as any what John Stuart Mill did when he called the earth "an odious scene of violence and tyranny." Still his instinctive faith in the goodness of living does not desert him. He knows pain? He resolves to weather it.

14

Heartbreak? He'll muddle through, somehow aware that dawn follows night. He knows that without bitterness there cannot be sweetness; without tragedy there cannot be joy. Life is precious precisely because it is precarious. And without death life would become unbearable.

The things that make life worth living are simple things, common things, things we may possess just by claiming them, though we can never own them; things we enjoy most when we share them with others. What are such things? Sunshine baking into one's flesh, the sting of rain on one's face, sharing a campfire with a congenial companion, feeling the rich glow of health after exertion, making a useful or beautiful object with one's own hands, receiving a cheery note from a distant friend, finding in a book the perfect expression of a thought for which one has long groped. The list is longer. Life offers the simpleton more than he or anyone else can ever fully appreciate or use up. What enriches his life most are unsophisticated pleasures, simple joys, which can neither be bought or sold, but can always be had for the asking and sharing.

> *"Rich in saving common sense,*
> *And, as the greatest only are,*
> *In his simplicity sublime."*
> — ALFRED LORD TENNYSON (1809-92)

11 BY POETRY, CONTEMPLATION, AND CHARITY

"The whole secret of remaining young in spite of years, is to cherish enthusiasm in one's self by poetry, by contemplation, by charity — that is, in fewer words, by the maintenance of harmony in the soul."
—HENRI FRÉDÉRIC AMIEL (1821-81)

At first reading this seems a curious recipe. Amiel could scarcely have chosen more unexpected words. Nothing about beauty parlors or travel to lands of romance — only three words, currently in disrepute. Poetry generally connotes a sentimental, impractical dilettantism; contemplation, a passive withdrawal from life's real concerns; and charity, condescension and the pauperizing of those to whom society denies justice. But this is not what Amiel meant.

By poetry Amiel meant whatever "pleasingly addresses the imagination, or embodies beautiful thought, feeling or action." The word stands for the whole realm of the imaginative, the intuitive, the imponderable. Science analyzes, isolates, measures, organizes; it deals with facts. But it has little to say about what Havelock Ellis called "the hardest of all facts — the facts of emotion."

By contemplation was meant what the dictionary says: "To contemplate is to look attentively; consider thoughtfully." Nothing mysterious or esoteric about this — just taking time to look, to probe below the surface, to know ourselves and our world a little better. One of the main reasons we grow old without attaining maturity is that we so seldom apply the grade-crossing slogan of yesteryear: "Stop! Look! Listen!"

Charity is a beautiful word. Just as "asylum" anciently meant "an inviolable shelter from arrest and punishment," so "charity" (the Latin *caritas*) meant Christian Love, love in the high sense of the thirteenth chapter of First Corinthians. Charity means to care. Amiel knew that nothing ages one so fast or surely as not to care deeply and sincerely for others. We should cherish enthusiasm; but we can do so only if we are willing to involve ourselves in the life of others.

"The function of poetry is clarification of life."

— ROBERT FROST (1874-1964)

"Men seek out retreats for themselves in the country, by the seaside, on the mountains, and thou too art wont to long above all for such things. But nowhere can a man find a retreat more full of peace than his own soul. Make use then of this retirement continually and regenerate thyself."

— MARCUS AURELIUS (121-180)

"Christianity taught us to care. Caring is the greatest thing; caring matters most."

— FRIEDRICH VON HUGEL (1852-1925)

"Everyone over twenty-five is an immigrant into a new world; only the young are native."
— MARGARET MEAD (1901-   )

The change our world is undergoing is much more radical than we have been able to comprehend. We have left the world of our childhood far behind. Many of us can remember when automobiles and telephones were scarce, and the delight we knew as children when the fire engines came clanging up the street behind the galloping stallions. Men have never before had to cope with a comparable amount of change within their own lifetimes. The rate of change, moreover, continues to accelerate. Our "knowledge explosion" forms a kind of chain reaction. There is literally no foretelling what sweeping transformation in the ways people experience life the rest of this century will bring.

So the question is not idle: how can we "immigrants" keep the resiliency and fortitude needed, in order to cope? How can we unlearn all that needs unlearning, because it is no longer relevant? We Americans have had a dream, the dream of a fully realized democracy. This was to be a society of the mutually concerned, a world where grown-ups really mature, and children are loved, and the doors of opportunity swing freely, and creativity is encouraged. "Religious democracy," Walt Whitman called it. Yet it seems as far away, or at least as unattainable as ever. Injustice remains entrenched. The roots of racism run deep. Like a giant octopus, the military establishment reaches out into our factories and schools and homes, setting up road-blocks preventing serious attack upon the cancerous sores that threaten the very life of our democracy.

Our job, like any immigrant's, is to do our damnedest to adjust — to learn the new language, the new ways; to overcome our fears; to focus our attention on the fast-arriving future, and keep on working to solve the problems besetting us. Whatever we can say about the past — and of course there is much that endears it to us — the most significant thing to say is that it is gone, and nothing can turn the clock back. The French poet, Théophile Gautier, once said:

"To be of one's own time — nothing seems easier and nothing is more difficult. One can go straight through one's age without seeing it, and this is what has happened to many eminent minds."

To be of our own time, to be brave-hearted, forward-looking immigrants in this new world, that is our job. It doesn't mean being sanguine about the future, or indifferent to its multiple dangers. It only means that it is our duty to be courageous, and, despite all temptation to despair, to hold firm our faith in man.

13   AS A TALE THAT IS TOLD

"The span of mortals is short, the end universal: and the tinge of melancholy which accompanies decline and retirement is in itself an anodyne. It is foolish to waste lamentation upon the closing phase of human life. Noble spirits yield themselves willingly to the successively falling shades which carry them to a better world or to oblivion."

— WINSTON CHURCHILL (1874-1965)

There is basic truth in the statement: "In the midst of life we are in death." Not only is there always death around us, never far away; there is death within us. For death is a continuous process that begins at birth. Many of the cells in our bodies live but for a few days; our oxygen-carrying red blood cells are particularly short-lived. Physically speaking, all of us dies repeatedly during our lifetimes.

We tend to think of life and death as contraries, as opposites. Not so. They belong together; one cannot have one without the other. Metabolism requires anabolism as well as catabolism. Only when the pump stops and the bellows cease, depriving the brain of oxygen-laden blood, does the final sleep come to the forebrain and we cease to be.

The individual is a microcosm of humanity. We are but cells in the great body, mankind. As was long ago observed: "Humanity lives only by the death of her servants, as we live by the decay and renewal of our bodies." We are a part of the vast metabolism that allows the evolution and renewal of the species, and that maintains the balance of nature, a balance jeopardized by science's success in lengthening our life span.

"Men do not deserve to suffer and die," wrote Camus, a man for whom I have profound admiration. But is it not just as meaningless to say man doesn't deserve to die as it would be to say he doesn't deserve to live? Against the suffering of others we should rebel, at least against needless, preventable suffering. But death is not our enemy, our "absurd destiny." It can come too soon, of course; many get short-changed. While we are blessed with health and capacity for enjoying life, we naturally want to postpone our hour of departure. Equally, death may come too late; too many linger on beyond their ability to enjoy, deprived of their dignity, even their identity.

But despite the fact that death sometimes intrudes prematurely, and sometimes tarries unconscionably, it is nontheless true that death is a necessity and in due season a blessing. Camus misread the story. Death doesn't make life meaningless; it makes it possible. The sting of transiency, moreover, gives life meaning as well as zest.

Still, man fears his own death. Heine spoke for many: "How our soul struggles against the thought of the cessation of our personality, of eternal annihilation." Even that sturdy scientist, Thomas Huxley, found that his dislike of the thought of extinction grew stronger as he neared the end of his days. We conclude that fear of death is a corollary of the love of life. "All my horror of dying," wrote Camus, "is contained in my jealous passion for life."

Can we not, then, conclude that there is no better antidote for the dread of death than a love of life, a well-cultivated capacity for enjoyment of these years that are let to us by that extraordinary, inexplicable providence that has caused life to sprout upon this lonely little planet? I am not happy with the prospect of my own departure. But when I analyze my feelings, I conclude with Montaigne that it is not death I fear, but dying. Dying can be painful and prolonged. But the chances are it will not be. Dying is usually more painful to watch than to experience.

In any case, we are mortal and it is the part of wisdom to sublimate our fear of death, to reconcile ourselves to it. Noble spirits do "yield themselves willingly to the successively falling shades which carry them to a better world or to oblivion."

"The laws of life and death are as they should be. The laws of matter and force are as they should be; and if death ends my consciousness, still is death good. I have had life on those terms, and somewhere, somehow, the course of nature is justified."
— JOHN BURROUGHS (1837-1921)

"By the word soul, or psyche, I mean that inner consciousness which aspires. By prayer I do not mean a request preferred to a deity; I mean . . . intense aspiration."

—RICHARD JEFFERIES (1848-87)

Let this be my prayer: that the sons of man shall be one at last, that the harmony of understanding and compassion shall triumph over the discords of suspicion and armament; that I may be part of the cure, not part of the world's sickness; one who seeks true community, true meeting; that I may love excellence, and hate shoddiness, duties shirked, and jobs half-done; that I may remember that they are many who hunger for warm rice, for milk and cheese, even a crust of stale bread; that they are many who long to be free, to go where they please, or to stay upon their own land; free to think, to laugh, to plan, to hope; that I may remember with loving concern those who call neighbor "stranger," who reject the world and dwell with suspicion and in loneliness; and those who, alien to themselves, know fear and despair; that I may remember all sorts and conditions of men: those naked to weather, helpless before torture, sick with guilt; those who are prisoner within the walls of tyrants, and the walls of indifference.

Remembering all such — remembering, too, the homes of happiness, the halls of learning and of healing, and the many whose lives are sun-sparkled and pleasant — may I know my involvement in mankind, and honor the claims of brotherhood, and accept the privilege and duty of serving as an instrument of the Love which is a partial reality, a "God" struggling for fuller birth.

"May the horizons of our mind be ever enlarged, until it shall include the great family here on earth with us, and those who have gone before and have left to us the heritage of their memory and of their work; and those whose lives will be shaped by what we do or leave undone."

— SAMUEL MCCHORD CROTHERS (1857-1927)

ON BEING TOTALLY ALIVE

"He was totally alive to all living things, and totally attentive to all persons."

— AUTHOR UNKNOWN

This was said of the great Negro scientist, George Washington Carver. It's about as fine a compliment as could be paid to anyone. What would it mean, we find ourselves asking, to be totally alive, truly aware of all the marvel and mystery embodied in the myriad forms of plant and animal life that forever surround us? Do we not inevitably spend many of our waking hours not completely awake? We cannot listen to all the noises that reach our eardrums, nor absorb all the sights and images that strike our eyes. Hardly aware that we are doing it, we select from the continuous stream of stimuli our senses bring to us. If the conversation is lively around the dinner table, we may scarcely know what we have eaten. If the mystery story is exciting, we may be quite oblivious to goings-on around us.

But if Buber was right that "all true living is meeting," we must beware lest this process of natural selection, this necessary art of "tuning out," cut us off from life and from experience. To be alive to all living things is to cultivate sensitivity and curiosity. It is to refuse to take even the most commonplace aspects of our experience for granted. A sense of wonder lies near the heart of true religiousness. The age of discovery doesn't lie somewhere in the past; not for us, anyway. There is ample ground for exploration, whether we are at home or abroad. The street where we have lived for years contains surprises, if we will look for them. Each new day offers enchanting possibilities. Trying to catch this sense of total aliveness I once wrote:

This of all moments is the moment —
The perfect instant, the quintessence
Of being, the golden conjunction
Of vanished yesterdays forever gone
And the ever-never arriving future.
Awake, my careless, open your eyes;
It will not return, it is all you have.
Yet in this briefest of all breaths,
This all is everything. It stands

21

Motionless, yet slips away
Before you look again, before you know.

Only this quick instant is mine.
But is it not enough, is it not
Sufficient? This incredible wonder
That now is now, and I am I, and love
Of all things real is realest, and of all
Things good is best — that love that flows
Like sunshine from the heart of being,
And warms my being till my heart would burst.

Why should my voice be still? Why should my eyes
Hide their astonishment? And why,
O why, should this glad heart of mine
Withhold its homage.

"Each day, as I look, I wonder where my eyes were yesterday."
— BERNARD BERENSON (1865-1959)

16   WORLD-AFFIRMATION

"And God saw everything that he had made, and behold, it was very good."

— GENESIS 1:31

In *The Golden Bough,* Sir James Frazer's monumental study of religions, he wrote:

"The saint and the recluse, disdainful of earth, and wrapt in ecstatic contemplation of Heaven, became in popular opinion the highest ideal of humanity . . . an obsession that lasted a thousand years."

Thus for at least half of Christian history, the gospel of Jesus has suffered grave and tragic distortion. Joshua ben Joseph, or as we name him, Jesus, was reared in the world-affirming faith of *The Book of Psalms* and the Hebrew prophets. Like the earlier prophets, the Nazarene found the plight of most men anguished and pain-filled. Raw and ugly suffering is a law of life; and man spends his years "as a tale that is told." Nevertheless, "the earth is the Lord's and the fullness thereof." Man does not properly give way to pessimism, cynicism, or despair.

Jesus accepted the Hebraic view of life, which draws no sharp distinction between the sacred and the secular. All things partake of holiness and are to be treated accordingly. He was no advocate of an impoverished life of disembodied spirituality, not he who is reported to have said: "I have come that men might have a more abundant life." So obvious was his enjoyment of living that he found himself accused of being a "glutton and a drunkard" and a friend of sinners. The author of *First Timothy* voiced Jesus' belief: "Everything created by God is good, and nothing is to be rejected if it is received with thanksgiving."

World-affirming religion, as Albert Schweitzer called it, does not allow the spiritual and the physical to be divorced. It holds it just as bad to be a spiritualist as to be a materialist. A creature of flesh and blood, man receives all experience through his ingenious sensory apparatus. His spiritual achievements are not disembodied. To play his music requires muscular strength and dexterity; his ideas must be given voice, or be translated into little ink-marks on paper. Without our senses, what could we know of beauty, truth, or love? That the human spirit has marvelous powers we perceive through the victory of a Helen Keller, who without eyes and ears yet learned to communicate. But we cannot conceive of a whole race so physically handicapped achieving much of anything.

It is good to be alive, which means to be embodied. For though I am not just my body, not just a few dollars' worth of common chemicals, I am not I without my body, without my brain and nervous system and the whole apparatus that allows me to experience the magic of movement and muscular harmony. It is good to be alive, a living organism, created out of the chemistry of the earth, a child of nature becoming articulate. To live is to let "the welter of the world pour through our senses."

This is not to advocate "eat, drink, and be merry, for tomorrow we die." Nor is it to deny that everything in life, however good in itself, is yet open to misuse. Human desires can and often do run rampant. Avarice, gluttony, and the other "deadly sins" are failures to regard the good gifts of earth as the means of promoting the life of man. But we do advocate that the physical and material side of life be given its proper place in one's scheme of things. The

23

right way to look at life is as a golden opportunity for a rich and happy experience in a world of beauty and plenty, where all things properly used can become the servants of man's character and fulfillment.

17 OUR SAFEST ELOQUENCE

"Our safest eloquence concerning God is our silence, when we confess that his glory is inexplicable, his greatness above our capacity and reach. He is above, and we upon earth; therefore it behooveth our words to be wary and few."

— THOMAS HOOKER (1586?-1647)

The English philosopher, L.P. Jacks, once described a friend: "He spent his breath in proving that God did not exist, but he spent his life in proving that he did." We have known atheists like that, just as we've known all too many whose lives have belied their pious professions of belief. If one has to choose between an atheistic iconoclast and an idolatrous believer, give us the former; ten-to-one, he would be more genuinely religious. How blasphemous is the attitude of those who refer to the Creator and Sustainer of this incredible universe as "The Friendly Man Upstairs!" If God is, rest assured, our proper feeling toward him is reverence and humility, and our words had best be "wary and few." If you are on terms of chatty familiarity with him, then it is not the God of the inter-galactic spaces you worship, but only a little tin-god of human manufacture. The divine is an abyss of mystery utterly transcending our momentary existence.

The search of God, for too many, results in a too-facile finding — a spurious finding, an overly-quick acceptance of a comforting word. The ordinary theist lays himself open to the charge of being, actually, an idolator. His belief in a little family-guardian of a god is like a Victorian lady's use of her parasol, to ward off the sun's blistering rays.

A young Hindu, studying in this country, went to a religious conference. Asked afterwards to give his impression of the meetings, he said: "I take it from what I heard that God is a Caucasian, an American, a Baptist, and a Republican." Most Christians think of Hinduism as idolatrous; but idolatry is not

24

limited to those who spin prayerwheels or kneel before graven images. Any man is an idolator as soon as he says glibly, "I worship God," really meaning only that he repeats well-worn phrases, and that he wants to reassure himself that God is on "his side" — his "maker, defender, redeemer and friend." It is all very human, this prevalent idolatry. This universe is too big for us: infinity and the *Mysterium Tremendum* are concepts with which we are still ill-equipped to cope. We cannot feel at home with them; we want a supernatural ally, a god whom we can understand and visualize, a god we can count on to help see us through.

It is important, but it is not easy, to outgrow idolatry. Thomas Hooker was right: "Our safest eloquence . . . is our silence."

"To whom then will ye liken God? or what likeness will ye compare unto him? . . . There is no searching of his understanding. . . All the nations are as nothing before him; they are counted to him as a thing of nought, and vanity."

— ISAIAH 40

18 HEALTHY SELFISHNESS

"My importance to the world is relatively small. On the other hand, my importance to myself is tremendous."

— NOEL COWARD (1899 -   )

It takes a pinch of humility to recognize just how unimportant to the world at large we are. We like to bolster our egos by pretending that what we are and do actually makes an appreciable difference, at least within a reasonable radius. The sobering truth is that, save for a tiny minority, the lives of men are not noticeably influential; few are long remembered after their deaths, or even missed after a few months by any save the small circle of family and intimate friends.

But though we are but single drops in the vast Mississippi of our race, we do need to feel important; and we can, in a perfectly legitimate way. We are important not to the world at large, but to the small world where we actually live. Our circle of influence is modest. The number of those who love us deeply and would miss us sorely we probably can count on the fingers of our hands. But in spite of this, it is quite possible to achieve a wholesome sense of our own selfhood, and find within ourselves that which can make life a satisfying and worthwhile experience.

There is much fuzziness in our thinking about selfishness. A moratorium on the use of the word might be a good idea. For all men are selfish; and all men ought to be selfish, if we mean by selfishness being important to oneself, and finding pleasure in one's own company. Selfishness can mean, of course, self-centeredness, an ingrown, imprisoning, engrossing concern for oneself that makes one incapable of love, of compassion, of generous and fair behavior. Nevertheless, each one of us is properly and inevitably the center of his own little world. Should we not admit in all honesty: My life, my unique experience — this is what genuinely counts most for me? My first job is to be myself. My primary responsibility is to take this gift of a life span and make something of it. Out of the womb of mother earth I am come; here I make my brief stand. And, if, as Thoreau put it, "I am not I, who will be?"

Since we have no way of living anybody else's life, let us recognize that there is a self-concern that is salutary and essential. Our primary task is to build meaning into our own lives, to fulfill so far as possible our potentialities; to be, in Maslow's term, "self-actualizing."

This, we acknowledge, is not what religious teachers have heretofore taught. They have urged men to be forgetful of self, to wage war upon the Ego; have preached the beauty of self-sacrifice, the need for self-denial, the ideal of self-surrender. Mystics have generally stressed that the way to know God is to follow the way of self-renunciation, the Via Negativa. I would argue that this is a tragic failure to differentiate between a healthy self-concern, such as Noel Coward voices, and an unhealthy self-preoccupation; between a proper pride and self-respect, and that self-inflation we call vanity, conceit, or arrogance.

Modern psychology has helped clarify this distinction. It has helped us understand that cockiness is not a sign of genuine self-assurance, that self-aggrandizement is but the outward mask of an inner emptiness and self-doubt. The blatant pride exhibited by a strutting Mussolini or psychopathic Hitler is but the false mask of a man who would hide from the world and himself his anxiety and self-hate. Contrariwise, gentleness is a sign not of weakness but of strength. Humility is genuinely experienced only by those sure

26

enough of their own worth to be able to live comfortably with the idea of their own relative insignificance.

It seems about time to re-evaluate the whole concept of selfishness. Let us call to the stand the extraordinary Dane, Kierkegaard:

"If anyone will not learn from Christianity to love himself in the right way, then neither can he love his neighbor . . . To love one's self in the right way and to love one's neighbor are absolutely analogous concepts, are at bottom one and the same . . . Hence the law is: 'You shall love yourself as you love your neighbor when you love him as yourself.'"

— SØREN KIERKEGAARD (1813-55)

19   TRUSTEES OF THREE SCORE YEARS AND TEN

We name you, but do not understand you. Those who say they know you, don't. Those who would turn from you, can't. When we think we cannot find you, we really mean we are looking at the wrong thing, or in the wrong way. Our conceptions of you, however well-intentioned, are misconceptions; our pictures of you are childish.

Yet you are self-evident, for you are reality — as simple, close, and inescapable as that. We look for you across the sea, while the ocean laps at our feet. We imagine you as one apart, as though you could be one object amongst many. We are like birds flying in search of air, like fish swimming in quest of water.

However inadequate, however idolatrous our thoughts, you are to us the love surrounding and sustaining us, the beauty gladdening and the truth liberating us. We cannot improve on Paul, telling the Athenians that the unkown god they worshipped in ignorance was indeed him in whom we live and move and have our being. Be then to us not an idol to be grasped, nor a magic name to be intoned, but simply life to be experienced, the mysterious, encouraging impulse deep within, impelling us to seek truth and to give our lives to love.

Once again we vacillators are seeking to renew our devotion to truth, our appreciation of beauty, our commitment to love. We confess we have been less than truthful with ourselves, blind to

27

beauty, and unmindful of the needs of others, even those of our own households. We have been guilty of thoughtlessness, enmeshed in trivia, forgetful of our own better insights. We have ignored our need for inward silence and serenity. We would not be so forgetful.

When we are tempted to act without thinking, to judge without knowledge, to condemn without cause, may remembrance of you restrain us, and hold us back from lying to ourselves and to others. May such remembrance help us to clarify our minds, straighten out our emotions, and keep us sane and decent in our dealings. Whatever else we do or fail to do, we should like to be worthy trustees of the three score years and ten you have given us to invest here on earth.

"Prayer is not . . . a magical device by which we get what we privately want, at the cost of the reliability of the natural order or the common good. Prayer is an intellectual discipline in truthfulness and a moral discipline in unselfishness. It is the endeavor to find what is true and right and then to conform to those realities."

— WILLARD SPERRY (1882-1954)

20   WHEN PATIENCE IS A VIRTUE

*"Patience is a virtue, possess it if you can.
'Tis seldom found in women, and never in a man."*

— ANONYMOUS

This old saw came to mind recently as I read a newspaper editorial calling for patience. This is a time especially calling for patience, said the writer. And I found myself pondering when patience really is a virtue and when it is not. Surely there are times when impatience is the virtue, when a man must refuse to acquiesce, when he must demand prompt action, and be unwilling to tolerate further delay. Having a good deal of the reformer in me, I am impatient with many things. So much needs changing, so many reforms are long over-due. Patience hasn't been one of my favorite virtues.

Still, to live successfully requires a lot of plain patience, the patience to persevere in the face of discouragement and defeat. A man without patience will eventually beat himself to pieces against the prison bars of his existence. Many things cannot be changed. One had best make peace with inevitables, for he is mortal, his energy and ability are subject to limitations. The road for everyman leads to decrepitude and bereavement and death. And this is something to which the wise person learns to be reconciled. Such reconcilement is not to be confused with apathy, or indifference to justice denied, or with that callousness that allows us to remain comfortably insulated from the suffering of others. Patience properly understood does not ask that we abandon the struggle to achieve international law and disarmament, and racial equality and an end of poverty at home. But just because these are proving exceedingly difficult goals to reach, we need patience, the kind Thomas Traherne long ago called "invincible patience." Invincible patience, he said, is closely akin to great courage and deep resolution.

Such invincible patience we do indeed need. Our nation has never been more dangerously divided, so full of angry voices, so much in need of citizens who will listen with sympathy and concern to those too impatient to tolerate further deferment of their aspirations. We need to hear those who are alarmed at the accelerating decline in the quality of the environment, and those militant extremists whose disillusionment has alienated them from much we take for granted and think we value. We must not meet impatience with impatience. Especially do those who are older need to be invincibly patient with a restless, reckless, rebellious younger generation, that flaunts its defiance of so much their elders have said they believed (however their actions have belied such belief). We older folks had best recognize that many of the young are serious-minded and truly searching for better answers than we have been able to give them. Many of them are committed and articulate, willing to be vulnerable, strong on freedom, contemptuous of hypocrisy. Their openness is refreshing, their eagerness for a more authentic life than they believe ours to be is admirable. We can well share their anguish in finding themselves in a world as bewildering and treacherous as ours — a world that tolerates racism, that has succumbed to militarism, and that reeks with hypocrisy and phoniness. We ought to share their disgust and exasperation with "the self-serving rhetoric" of our society.

When is patience a virtue? Most of all in troubled days like these. But always is it needed, needed as perceptive listening, as the resolute determination to understand what others are trying to communicate. Even as a young mother must have invincible patience with her bawling babe, refusing to get angry and insisting on learning instead what is the cause of all this grief, so must we listen to the strident voices of today in a way that can help bring as prompt a correction of wrongs, as prompt a meeting of proper needs and demands as is humanly possible.

"From the murmur and subtlety of suspicion with which we vex one another, give us rest. Make a new beginning. And mingle again the kindred of the nations in the alchemy of love; and with some finer essence of forbearance temper our minds."—

ARISTOPHANES (448?-385? B.C.)

21 THE TRUTH OF IMAGINATION

"I am certain of nothing but of the holiness of the heart's affections and the truth of imagination."

— JOHN KEATS (1795-1821)

No one in his right mind would seek to belittle the achievements of science; but we have expected of science more than it can produce. It can serve, but cannot save. "Pure intellect," Emerson said a century before we split the atom, "is the pure devil." Indeed, it may be. A savage armed with facts is still a savage; Genghis Khan plus atom bombs is but evil compounded.

In concentrating upon the scientific avenue to truth, men since the Renaissance have seriously neglected the complementary avenue suggested by the poet — "the truth of imagination." Certainly, intuitive truth can mislead, is far from infallible. But somehow, centuries before the scientists, men like Buddha and Jesus, Aristotle and Socrates lived and gave the world excellent guidance.

Imagination, says the dictionary, is the constructive or creative faculty. While "fancy flits about the surface and is airy and playful, sometimes false, imagination is deep, essential, spiritual. It goes to the heart of things, and is earnest, serious, and seeks always and everywhere for essential truth."

The wisdom of the heart's surmise must always be checked against the facts the mind discovers. But knowledge is not wisdom. Because we are spiritual beings, we need poetry and music, we need beauty. We need to keep alert to life's overtones, attuned to those "authentic tidings of invisible things" of which another poet speaks.

A doctor we know prescribes this cure for headaches: let the patient relax comfortably, eyes lightly closed; and let him think, quietly but intensely, about the loveliest place he knows. He must use his imagination, create the scene, make it vivid, detailed; he must concentrate upon it, and, in a few minutes, five or ten at most, the headache will be gone.

I have no license to practice medicine, and am not recommending this as a cure for headaches. But I do recommend it as a valuable technique for developing both concentration and the power of imagination.

> *"A thing of beauty is a joy forever;*
> *Its loveliness increases; it will never*
> *Pass into nothingness; but will keep*
> *A bower quiet for us, and a sleep*
> *Full of sweet dreams, and health, and quiet breathing."*
> — KEATS

22   THE DEEP POWER IN WHICH WE EXIST

"There is a deep power in which we exist and whose beatitude is accessible to us. Every moment when the individual feels himself invaded by it is memorable. It comes to the lowly and simple; it comes to whosoever will put off what is foreign and proud; it comes to us as insight; it comes as serenity and grandeur. The soul's health consists in the fullness of its reception."
—RALPH WALDO EMERSON (1803-82)

My heart confirms the truth of these words. This confirmation does not rest on some exalted mystical experience, but upon my encounters with men of good will, on my response to the astonishing beauty of nature, on my sense of the goodness of being. We find ourselves at home in this world, despite its appalling tragedies and evils. These anger us, because they forever

31

threaten the values we cherish. We cannot explain the existence of evil in the world. We only know that we are called upon to fight it, to "overcome evil with good." Whatever freedom we believe we have in life, we are not free to abandon the struggle to make our planet a place where children can thrive, where the doors of opportunity are equally open, where hunger and poverty are banished, where war is replaced by a just reign of law, and where man's knowledge and rich heritage are accessible to all.

Where the world came from we do not know; nor can we read the future. But the world does provide a setting for the growth of spirit, a gymnasium for the development of values, a studio for the further creating of beauty. Something, clearly, some mysterious power of intelligence, of excellence, and benevolence, is at work in nature and in our hearts. Many nowadays may feel reluctant to call this something "God." There is much to be said for not labeling it too hastily. Things we label we think we understand. Still the poet, Paul Engle, testifies:

"You say you've buried God (weeping you say it)
And split the flesh to its essential parts,
But you have left us bodies bright with flame
And buried God no deeper than our hearts."

This "God" we discover buried in our own hearts is not, assuredly, the old Cosmic Ally. This is a very different conception of deity. It seems of little importance whether we call it by one name or another. But it *is* important that we do not fail to ponder what this "deep power in which we exist and whose beatitude is accessible to us" can mean to us; that we do not fail to ask: What is it that makes me feel dissatisfied with ugliness, that forces me to protest any attack upon the dignity of man? What is it to which I should give my allegiance, that makes me respond to the claims of conscience, compassion, and understanding? How does it happen that love — the reaching out of the human spirit in tenderness and concern to others — seems supremely important to me?

Call it what you will: Reality, Nature, God, or Sanctity in Existence, the Ground of All Being, the Sum of All Good. The important thing is to keep ourselves open to wonder, sensitive to beauty, responsive to conscience and the tug of ideals, and committed to truth, to justice, and to love.

NATURE'S IMPARTIAL PROVIDENCE

"I see on an immense scale, and as clearly as in a demonstration in a laboratory, that good comes out of evil; that the impartiality of the Nature Providence is best; that we are made strong by what we overcome; that man is man because he is as free to do evil as to do good; that life is as free to develop hostile forms as to develop friendly; that power waits upon him who earns it; that disease, wars, the unloosened, devastating elemental forces have each and all played their part in developing and hardening man and giving him the heroic fiber."

— JOHN BURROUGHS (1837-1921)

This beloved old naturalist did not attempt to solve the problem of evil, or to by-pass it. But he thought he could see this much light, that "the impartiality of the Nature Providence is best." And isn't it? What better plan can be conceived for an experiment whose purpose is growth, not stagnation, and freedom rather than a totally determined life? Let us not minimize the mystery of evil, or make light of the cruel yoke of human suffering. Evil is evil, and ugly. But assuming that growth and freedom are indispensable to any existence we could characterize as worth having, we too can affirm that nature's strict impartiality is indeed best. A perfect world would be like the conventional image of heaven — a boring, static place, quite unacceptable to a species like man.

The historian, Charles A. Beard, used to speak of what he called "the calamity theory of progress." On the basis of historical evidence he argued that progress springs from tragedy. The newly launched, supposedly invincible Titanic sinks, and at last men devise an international iceberg reporting system. The Great Depression grips the country, causing untold misery, and at last men work out a more humane way of protecting the old, the sick, the unemployed against financial disaster. Perhaps only major calamities can teach men how they must be their brother's keeper.

To be sure, this leaves us less than satisfied. It offers scant comfort to the passenger on the Titanic, or the dispossessed Dust Bowl farmer. But it does do something important. Whoever accepts fully the idea of nature's impartiality learns to look on evil in a less-tortured way. Evil remains unexplained, but God is not to blame, nor his love called into question. Gone is the need to wrestle with the insoluble dilemma, that if God be all-powerful, then his character is defective, while if he be perfect goodness, he must labor under inscrutible limitations. However dimly, we apprehend that evil plays a necessary role, that "good comes out of evil, that we are made strong by what we overcome."

"The most important lesson that man can learn from his life is not that there is pain in this world, but that it depends upon him to turn it into good account, that it is possible for him to transmute it into joy."

—RABINDRANATH TAGORE (1861-1941)

24 LIVING IN CREATION'S DAWN

"I used to envy the father of our race, dwelling as he did in contact with the new-made fields and plants of Eden; but I do so no more because I have discovered that I also live in 'creation's dawn.' The morning stars still sing together, and the world, not yet half made, becomes more beautiful every day."

— JOHN MUIR (1838-1914)

The idea of ought looms large in religion. Religion is thought to be a duty, an obligation, a matter of obedience to divine edict. No reasons are offered in support of the Ten Commandments save one: "I am the Lord thy God." It's as simple as that. God says, as human fathers are wont to tell their small fry: "Do as you are told. Don't ask why, just obey me." For the ancient Hebrew as for the modern Orthodox Jew, religion is very much a "command performance." He is even commanded to love God. Surely if a man believes in God, the appropriate attitude to take toward him is not cowering fear. But love is something which must be freely given; it can be offered and invited, but it cannot be made compulsory. Micah's "What doth the Lord require of thee, but to do justly, and to love mercy, and to walk humbly with thy God" lists three primary virtues. But is a man to be just, merciful, and humble because he is *required* to be, or of his own free will?

So deeply ingrained was this idea of religion as "command performance" in Judaism, that it carried right over into Christianity. Jesus protested against the legalism of the Pharisees, proclaiming that the Sabbath was made for man. But when he taught, "Judge not," he added, "for with what judgment ye judge, ye shall be judged." We should forgive, but why? So that God will forgive us. "If ye forgive not men their trespasses, neither will your Father forgive your trespasses." How tragic to reduce living to this kind of transactional basis.

A person should be able to say: "I love, I honor, I forgive, I speak the truth, I will not kill or steal or be unfaithful, covetous or idolatrous, because this is the way I want to live. I want to do what I am persuaded is right, neither to get into heaven, nor for any other reward save the inner satisfaction that grows out of self-respect and integrity."

Let us be good because we take delight in being good. Let us heed the great commandments of old, not because they are divine commands, but because our study of the consequences of human behavior amply demonstates their soundness as principles to govern action. Let us tell the truth, so that the clarity of truth may dwell within us. Let us love our fellowman, because love is the first thing and the last thing — because the satisfactions of loving are sufficient unto themselves.

Einstein put the sense of awe and wonder at the center of true religiousness; let us also. Let us learn never to take anything for granted; never to let a blade of grass become a commonplace, or a beetle less than a "walking miracle." Let us never forget how wonderfully and fearfully we are made. And let us remember that "the morning stars still sing together, and the world, not yet half made, becomes more beautiful every day."

"How wondrously strange, and how miraculous is this! I draw water, I carry fuel."
— A ZEN BUDDHIST SAYING

25 LONELINESS AND TOGETHERNESS

"No man is an Iland, intire of itselfe; every man is a peece of the Continent, a part of the maine; if a Clod bee washed away by the Sea, Europe is the lesse ... as well as if a Mannor of thy friends or of thine owne were; any man's death diminishes me, because I am involved in Mankinde; And therefore never send to know for whom the bell tolls; it tolls for thee."

— JOHN DONNE (1573-1631)

Generations have loved these words. They voice with beauty a profound truth: we are members one of another. There is no true isolation. Yet there is a complementary truth. With equal pertinency, cannot the individual be likened to an island, forever separated from every other living being? Who has not felt loneliness, the sense of being isolated even from nearest and dearest? We recall Matthew Arnold's "Isolation:"

"Yes! in the sea of life en-isled,
With echoing straits between us thrown,
Dotting the shoreless watery wild,
We mortal millions live alone."

The poet imagines that the islands cry out in despair against this separation, and long to be once more "parts of a single continent."

"Who rendered vain their deep desire!
A God, a God their severance ruled!
And bade betwixt their shores to be
The unplumb'd, salt estranging sea."

Despite man's gregariousness, there is this sense in which we are utterly alone. Love builds its bridges; there is a friendly traffic between our shores. But we are individuals, unique, and forever held apart. If God commands this severance, we think it for some purpose. Augustine begins his *Confessions:* "Our hearts are restless." Perhaps if we lived in humanity as completely as bees belong to a hive or ants to their colony, our hearts would not be restless and hence not driven to seek God.

Both Arnold and Donne proclaim essential truths. We are lonely and possessed by unspeakable longings; and these, we think, awaken our need of God and make us restless searchers. But even as the islands that dot the bay are in reality part of the mainland, being joined through the ocean bottom, so are we, in a profoundly true sense, knit together, woven into one fabric.

THE EMPEROR AND THE BUSYBODY

"Begin the morning by saying to thyself, I shall meet with the busybody, the ungrateful, arrogant, deceitful, envious, unsocial. All these things happen to them by reason of their ignorance of what is good and evil. But . . . I can neither be injured by any of them, nor can I be angry with my kinsman nor hate him. For we are made for cooperation, like feet, like hands. To act against one another, then, is contrary to nature; and it is acting against one another to be vexed and to turn away."

— MARCUS AURELIUS (121-180)

It is comforting to know that the imperial sage met the busybody. Any man in power is peculiarly beset by persons who see in his prestige and influence means to their own ends. Whether we live in a palace, then, or in the humblest home, we shall meet the vexatious person. And it is at this point that our belief in human brotherhood faces a trying test. It costs nothing to believe in brotherhood in the abstract. But how about the neighbor who borrows but does not return, who talks but does not listen, who takes but never gives? We have difficulty remembering that the road-hog is our brother, as is also a long-winded usurper of our party line. We should indeed begin the morning by resolving not to be vexed by such as these. It is of such persons, perhaps, that Jesus thought when he warned: "Judge not, that ye be not judged."

Living in society involves wear and tear; we must expect interruptions, delays, petty frustrations. And we must particularly beware lest, becoming annoyed at others, we allow ourselves to be dragged down to their level. "The best way of avenging thyself," said Marcus Aurelius, "is not to become like the wrongdoer. Men exist for the sake of one another. Teach them, then, or bear with them."

"It is no great matter to associate with the good and gentle; for this is naturally pleasing to all, and everyone willing enjoyeth peace, and loveth those best that agree with him. But to be able to live peaceably with hard and perverse persons, or with the disorderly, or with such as go contrary to us, is a most commendable and manly thing."

— THOMAS A KEMPIS (1380-1471)

ON BEING RELIGIOUSLY TONGUE-TIED

"Whoever come to Me, through whatsoever form, I reach them. All men are struggling through paths which in the end lead to me."
—THE BHAGAVAD-GITA (500-200 B.C.)

It is unfortunate that so many regard religious statements as informational, as presenting facts, when their function is not that at all. When a poet writes of a "shot heard around the world," we have no difficulty in interpreting his metaphor. The American Revolution *was* news that ultimately penetrated lands far away. As Rabbi Abraham Cronbach has observed, our "objections to religious statements — entirely valid objections when those statements are used informationally — cease to be valid once the non-informational import of those statements is recognized."

The scientist in his laboratory, the philosopher in his text, the teacher before his class, the witness under oath in court, are all under obligation to speak as factually and accurately as they can. But the poet's obligation to speak truly and truthfully is of another dimension. He voices feelings, strives to give life wings, to announce that which is no less real because it surpasses literal conceptions.

Forgetting this distinction, our generation has increasingly become religiously tongue-tied. The older language of religious devotion filled with anthropomorphic imagery is found embarrassing. It threatens our intellectual integrity. At least we think it does. So when we try, if we try at all, to speak to God, we find ourselves talking in vague philosophic abstractions. We cannot make God real to ourselves, or close, or important. Yet if we are to live religiously, appreciatively, trustingly, and sensitively — we need language that can evoke our feelings.

Someone has said that without poetry mankind would never have learned much about love. We usually think of it the other way round. Perhaps; but equally, possibly more basically, because men have written poetry, they have discovered how much more than sexual desire is involved in love: tenderness, continuing concern, spiritual communion, the uncalculating affirmation of another human being. By developing a language of love, the race has gradually learned not only how to express its profounder feelings, but equally how to awaken them.

Even so with the language of religion. That which we cannot somehow put into words, we cannot adequately feel. What we do not express we soon lose the capacity to experience. Many speak today of God as absent, exiled, even dead. What they really seem to mean is that they have lost their power to talk to or about him meaningfully.

God cannot be defined, being by definition beyond human conceptualization. That's really our problem: How can we conceive the inconceivable? James Martineau suggests what seems the best solution:

"All belief and speech respecting God is untrue yet infinitely truer than any non-belief and silence. The confession of ignorance once made, we may proceed to use such poor thought and language as we find least unsuitable to so high a matter."

28 A DREAM

"God keeps up a continual conversation with every human creature."

— PAUL CLAUDEL (1868-1955)

I dreamed
And in my dream I seemed to hear God's Voice,
Answering the universal chorus of pater nosters
Rising unceasingly from the earth.
And the Voice said:
"My children on earth,
You worship me with your lips,
But it is your hearts that I desire.
You pray for my kingdom,
But it cannot come until you learn to do justly
And to love mercy and to walk in harmony with my laws.
I have made you trustees of the earth:
Till its soil,
Guard its fertility, the purity of its water
And blanket of air.
Reap its harvests and distribute its bounty
To those who hunger,
And you shall have bread all your days.
Forgive one another,

And you will not need my forgiveness,
Since you will be able then to forgive yourselves.
To live is to know temptation —
Temptation to good no less than to evil.
For I have made you free,
And but little less than divine,
Able to choose good and to resist evil.
Therefore,
Overcome evil with good.
So shall you become citizens of my kingdom,
And share in my glory,
Forever."
The Voice ceased,
And in my dream I looked at my fellowmen,
And their lips were moving in prayer.
But I saw that much speaking
Had made them deaf.

"Stop and step a little aside, out of the noisy crowd and incumbering hurry of the world, and calmly take a prospect of things . . . After we have made just reckonings, we shall begin to think the world in great measure mad, and that we have been in a sort of Bedlam all this while."

—WILLIAM PENN (1644-1718)

29 THE HEARTBEAT OF LIFE

"Everything the true hasid does or does not do mirrors his belief that, in spite of the intolerable suffering men must endure, the heartbeat of life is holy joy, and that always and everywhere, one can force a way through to that joy — provided one devotes one's self entirely to his deed."

— MARTIN BUBER (1878-1965)

I believe this, too. Don't ask me to prove it, for of course I cannot, any more than could the hasidic Jew. Life is not something to be argued with. The world is. Time out of mind this spinning speck has carried on its rhythmic dance about the sun. We are creatures of a moment; tomorrow will not know us. Of the whys and wherefores of the universe we know precisely nothing. How life arose from the primeval hot thin soup in the Archaeozoic ooze remains a mystery. We only know we are, the world is; and that everywhere we walk, we stumble into mystery and confront beauty.

Against human mis-administration there is point in rebelling, but it makes no sense to argue with the breeze in the pine trees, the laughter of a mountain stream, or the Milky Way on whose perimeter we ride. There the only wisdom is acquiescence, a yea-saying response.

Alas, we see the world as it truly is only to the degree that we allow ourselves to see it. The person at war with himself, refusing to accept himself as he is, cannot accept the world as it is. His own inner distortions are reflected in the way he interprets reality. Meanwhile, a Helen Keller, deprived of sight and hearing, was able to achieve a deep appreciation of the world around her. Imprisoned in dark silence, she responded to life with a psalm of gratitude and praise. The world seems to mirror back to us our own image of ourselves. What we see "out there" is colored by what we feel "in here." If the universe seems empty and meaningless, this may be symptomatic of our own sense of hollowness and insignificance.

The man at home with himself finds the universe homelike. He who is his own good friend meets a friendly world. He who loves himself properly has little trouble loving his neighbor or his God. His attitude is that of the humble Einstein, who confessed in his *Mein Weltbild:*

"Many times a day I realize how much my own outer and inner life is built upon the labors of my fellowmen, both living and dead, and how earnestly I must exert myself in order to give in return as much as I am able."

No man is self-made; everyone is a debtor to fellowman and to providential nature. The humility of an Albert Einstein or a John Q. Citizen grows out of a mature recognition and acceptance of the role of receiver of more than one can ever hope to give.

"The heartbeat of life is holy joy." We can only assert it, never for a moment forgetting that the suffering men must endure does often seem intolerable. But to find our way to that joy is not always easy, since it involves nothing less than making peace with ourselves.

41

"Perhaps in time I shall learn to live more deeply and consistently in that undistracted center of being where will does not intrude, and the sense of time passing is lost, or has no power over the imagination."

— KATHERINE ANNE PORTER (1894-   )

Say to yourself: Be still. Grow Quiet. Forego for awhile the active tense. Let nature's calm enfold you. Graciously accept the fact you are alive. What wonder is this, that conscious, sentient life is yours, that creation should become aware of itself in you?

Now feel the steady pulse, the wheeling of the heavens, the turning of the earth, the tidal ebb and flow, the rhythm of day and night, seed-time and harvest. Inwardly rejoice in being part of nature. Inhale these winds of mystery. Wonder at the abyss of space, and wonder also at the abyss of being you encounter within yourself.

Stop. Look. Listen.

Stop doing long enough to be, to know what being is.

Look long enough really to see.

Listen long enough to let life speak to you.

Heed what you have to say to yourself. Find out what you truly want. But how? Still the clamorous messages of the senses, the insistent demands of the surface mind. Cease from your childish games, your vain pursuits, your merry-go-rounding. Be still. Grow quiet. Wait. Wait for your inmost self to speak. Wait till you see what you must do, what your true priorities are. Wait till you know what idols to dethrone, and what God you will worship, in spirit and in truth.

"In the midst of Silence a secret word was spoken to me."

— WILLIAM BLAKE (1757-1827)

31   THE SCIENCE OF HONESTY AND GOODNESS

"All other knowledge is hurtful to him who has not the science of honesty and goodness."

— MONTAIGNE (1533-92)

Day by day our papers bring us ill-tidings — of wars in Indo-China and the Middle-East; of crime and corruption, famines and race riots. Our world is sick, our civilization threatened with annihilation, not for want of knowledge but for want of enough honesty and goodness. The cultivation of personal integrity and character in such a time may seem unimportant. It is not the world, however, but men — ourselves — who are unskilled in this basic science.

What can I, a lone individual, do? How often we ask this, in genuine frustration. Would that we had wisdom and power to remold the world. But how seldom we go on from there, take the next step — an acknowledgment that the truly honest, thoroughly good man does have an almost unbelievable influence.

"One man in the power of God can shake the countryside for ten miles around." So said George Fox, the early Friend. Ten miles? He shook all England. And another, in our day, by making his life "an apprenticeship to truth," and by achieving a radical goodness — I mean Gandhi — freed one-fifth of the human race, and showed mankind a new kind of war, "war without violence." Compile your own list: Schweitzer, Jane Addams, Martin Luther King; and those others, without fame, whom you yourself have known, influencing other lives for good and sweetening the community.

However average his abilities, the man who really tackles the job of becoming proficient in "the science of honesty and goodness" becomes part of that precious yeast which alone can leaven the world.

"Another parable spake he unto them; the kingdom of heaven is like unto leaven, which a woman took, and hid in three measures of meal, till the whole was leavened."
— MATTHEW 13:33

Let me have such reverence for life, such devotion to truth, such compassion for fellowman, and such confidence in myself, as will enable me to play my part like a man. Let me discover goodness in others and how to encourage it, and mercy in myself and how to show it. Let me awaken to fuller knowledge of our human oneness, and how to act upon it.

32 NEVERTHELESS

*"When everything holy was throughout the land being destroyed
or profaned, this chapel was built to the glory of God by Sir
Robert Shirley, Baronet, whose singular praise it was to have done
the best things in the worst times, and hoped for them in the most
calamitous."*

—INSCRIPTION IN A CHURCH, LEICESTER, ENGLAND 1653

Sorrow is everywhere, yet joy is reborn. The alarums of war are
thunderous and there seems no end to tragic human waste.
Nevertheless, people still find peace in their hearts, beauty in the
world, and love and happiness in their families and in their
friendships. Evil remains rampant, mediocrity prevails,
disappointments abound. Yet are there men of honor, and
cherishers of excellence. Again and yet again the heart sees
heroism displayed, and knows once more the reality of rectitude.

There is much evil in the world. Let us do good. Dishonesty
often seems the best policy. Let us be scrupulously honest. Strife
tears our world apart. Let us continue to hope for peace, and to
work for it. Let us love and not hate, build and not destroy. Let us
be true to our ideals, and hold fast our faith that in all and around
all and above all is One who is just and true.

"This is the vision of a great and noble life:
to endure ambiguity in the movement of truth
and to make light shine through it;
to stand fast in uncertainty;
to prove capable of unlimited love and hope."

— KARL JASPERS (1883-1969)

33 MEETING THE WORLD DIVINELY

*"I have a hundred times wished that if God upheld nature He
would mark the fact unequivocally, but that if the signs which she
gives of a God are fallacious, she would wholly suppress them, that
she would either say all or nothing, that I might see what part I
should take . . . Truly Thou art a God that hidest thyself."*

—BLAISE PASCAL (1623-62)

Many an honest man has shared this mystical mathematician's disquiet, torn between faith and doubt, finding some evidence of a Creator, "too much to deny yet too little to affirm." The dilemma stems, in part, from the use of the indefinite article "a." If you say "a God," you make god an object, one amongst many, an infinitely superior person or intelligence; and there is no conclusive evidence for the existence of such an entity. Paul Tillich used to put it that while God may not *exist,* he *is.* God, that is, is not a being, but Being Itself. John Burroughs gave us one of the best and clearest of such statements, in his *Accepting the Universe:*

"God is the fact of the fact, the life of the life, the soul of the soul, the incomprehensible, the sum of all contradictions, the unit of all diversity; he who knows him, knows him not; he who is without him, is full of him; turn your back upon him, then turn your back upon gravity, upon air, upon light. He cannot be seen; but by him all seeing comes. He cannot be heard, yet by him all hearing comes. He is not a being, yet apart from him there is no being — there is no apart from him."

This points the way around Pascal's dilemma. Subtracting man from nature, we have no unequivocal testimony. But it is neither necessary nor right to subtract man from nature. Man *is* nature at one of its levels. We ourselves constitute telling evidence concerning the nature of ultimate reality. Our seeking for righteousness, our striving for truth and justice and love, our insatiable hunger for God are a pertinent part of the testimony.

"The proof of . . . my God-idea is this: that in meeting my world divinely it shows itself divine. It supports my postulate. And without such an act of will, no discovery of divinity could take place . . . Impute then to the world a living beneficence: the world will not reject this imputation . . . He who waits his assents till God is proved to him, will never find Him. But he who seeks finds — has already found."

— WILLIAM ERNEST HOCKING (1873-1966)

"My atheism, like that of Spinoza, is true piety toward the universe and denies only gods fashioned by men in their own image, to be servants of their human interests."
— GEORGE SANTAYANA (1863-1952)

What a sentence! Most atheists have been less urbane. They have generally been militant debunkers of "gods fashioned by men in their own image, to be servants of their human interests." This utilitarian conception of deity has been all too prevalent through the ages, and any man who believes in a personal god had best examine to make sure his conception isn't a gross impiety toward the universe.

Santayana wrote this sentence long before the ecological crisis became a household phrase. Who had even heard of ecology in 1922? Now man's impiety toward the universe is plainly bringing disaster. Our impiety has made most American rivers open sewers; we foul the air we breathe with billions of tons of carbon dioxide pumped into the atmosphere annually. Even the oceans are threatened. If man's crunching of nature, his fouling of the earth, and his over-breeding are not soon checked, he will starve, or suffocate, or drown in his own garbage. Such words might have seemed alarmist a few years back. Now few thoughtful men are like to so consider them.

Whether one is an atheist or a true believer, one had better be an ardent conservationist. Albert Schweitzer's "reverence for life," all life, not just human life, makes better sense all the time. Such reverence is indeed the cornerstone of ethics. The brotherhood of man, so far from realized, is still not enough; the religious person must also preach and practice a more-than-human brotherhood. We used to hear much about isolationsim; many Americans hoped we could keep our nation uninvolved in the affairs of other nations. That sort of isolationism is happily a thing of the past. But there is another kind men need to outgrow: that provincialism that lets them regard their species as the central focus of value, all other forms of life on the planet existing only for man's benefit. Indeed, most of us two-leggeds have difficulty imagining that other creatures have rights, or even any value save as they contribute to our well-being, by feeding us or giving us some aesthetic satisfaction, or, more vaguely, by helping to maintain the balance of nature.

If man must rule the earth, let him realize that with power goes responsibility. If he is bound to manipulate nature, then let him also learn to control himself. If he *will* play god, then let him learn to be a beneficient deity. Let him be trustee and guardian of the whole, wondrous web of life, the entire biotic community.

For all our talk, our noble speeches, man's "silent war" on nature continues. But unless a lasting "cease-fire" is soon achieved, Rachel Carson's "silent spring" will be a full reality, for no one will be left to sing that plaintive folk song of our time: "Where have all the flowers gone?"

35   AN ACCOUNTING OF GRATITUDE

"The grateful soul of the wise man is the true altar of God."
—PHILO JUDAEUS (c. 20 B.C.-c.50 A.D.)

I say to myself: Be thankful.

Be thankful for the happiness you have known in times past, the moments of mirth and ecstasy, the years of health. How many of your dreams have come true; promises, long deferred, have so often at last been made good.

Be thankful for the dearness of your loved ones, the fidelity of your friends, the courtesy and kindness repeatedly shown you by total strangers.

Be thankful that your fears have again and again proven groundless, that you have survived so many close calls, so many narrow escapes; and that the same good fortune has generally followed your children in their misadventures, and your friends likewise.

Be thankful not only for the joys that have accompanied your way, and the unnumbered gifts of a kindly providence. Master the harder art of gratitude for life's sterner lessons. You have known pain, pain that has given you warning of unseen dangers. You have known failure, failure that shattered false hopes of easy victory, and toughened your spirit for renewed efforts. Having made mistakes, you have learned important lessons. Having encountered obstacles, you have found courage and endurance to surmount them. Having known sorrow and loneliness, you have discovered that even these have quickened your sympathy, and taught you your need of others.

Be thankful, then, that so much you have not sought and would have by-passed if you could, nonetheless has proved enriching to your experience. Even in life's dark labyrinthine ways and bitter moments, the man of faith and hope can trace the workings of a mysterious wisdom, an impartial providence, a more than human love.

36   ON DOING WHAT COMES UNNATURALLY

"The never-ending task of finishing himself, of transcending the limits of his phyiscal being, is the powerhouse of man's creativeness and the source of his unnaturalness."

— ERIC HOFFER (1902-   )

A part of nature, man stands curiously apart from the rest of nature. Alone of earth's creatures, he refuses to play the game by nature's rules. Some itch in his head — we call it intelligence — makes him unwilling just to do what comes naturally. Hence he is, in Pascal's phrase, "the glory, and the scandal, of the universe."

In a world of many wonders, few things are more wonderful than instinct. By it animals prosper, knowing what to eat, what to avoid, how to build a nest or burrow, who are their natural enemies, who their friends. Most of the birds that in summer throng our northern woods migrate in fall to warmer lands. By instinct the ant and the bee establish great colonies where order prevails — cities without crime, slums, proverty and pollution.

But man declines to give unquestioning obedience to his natural instincts. This does indeed make him scandalous, a disturber of nature's balanced scheme. His insatiable craving for novelty, pleasure, and power has now brought him to the point where he threatens the very future of the globe. As our ecological crises deepen, we shall better understand how deeply man must pay for riding rough-shod over instinct. War, that most unnatural of human pursuits, makes us bipeds worse than scandalous; our worship of Mars will shortly finish us off, man and beast alike, unless renounced, once and for all.

But there is also the other side of this equation, the glory side, and it is misanthropic to forget it. It does seem unlikely that man can sufficiently redress the imbalance of nature his ingenuity and technology have brought about to save himself and the planet. But then, nothing about man is one bit likely. This much seems certain, as long as man endures, his role will continue to be both part of nature and also *more* than nature. Millenia ago our distant ancestors passed "the point of no return." Since then, our race has had no choice but to struggle on along the road toward manhood.

Man is an unfinished creature whose eternal task is transcending his animal ancestry. Defying nature's ironclad rules, he achieves something very precious; a measure of freedom. We speak of animals being free: actually, their "freedom" is illusory. The big cat in the jungle may seem freer than the tiger in the zoo, but he is not. He is happier, no doubt, because able to behave according to his tiger nature; but freedom is not a matter of the absence of bars. It is having real choices to make. Nothing accentuates the distinction between human and non-human nature more clearly than man's aspiration toward freedom in a universe of undeviating law, a world that apart from man seems totally determined.

Ours is a limited freedom. We carry our instinctual heritage deep within us, and it determines most of what we are and feel and do. But the small margin of our freedom is enough to give us opportuntiy to become more than we are, to make real decisions, and to express whatever uniqueness and creativity we may happen to possess.

There are those, especially among today's younger generation, who advocate our going "back to nature." But who would really want to? Any return to nature would involve abandoning freedom. Man's task of finishing himself requires that the innovator be encouraged, the right to be different protected. Consider the unnaturalness of art. The artist does not seek to copy nature, but to improve upon the natural. Or, as Paul Klee put it, "Art does not reproduce the visible; rather it makes visible." When the first man chipped a stone into an arrowhead or other artifact, he became an artist. By artificial we usually mean something "not genuine." But the primary meaning of artificial is simply something made by human skill and labor, rather than by nature. We compliment a person by calling him "natural," meaning unaffected. But man's glory lies precisely in his ability to create what isn't found in nature, his insistence on doing what doesn't come naturally.

Not only is art artificial, but so is science and technology. What could be more artificial than an automobile, or than the contraption at which I sit typing these words? How thoroughly artificial is language, an artificiality that seldom strikes us until we undertake to master a foreign tongue? When Pope Paul condemns birth control as being "artificial," contrary to nature, he sounds like those who once condemned anesthesia for the same reason. Such condemnation logically should apply to all civilization, all governments and institutions, including that marvelous human fabrication over which the Pope himself presides.

To condemn man for doing what is unnatural is really to renounce the whole human venture. Man's job is not to return to nature — an utter impossibility. It is to complete himself, transcend himself, become much more fully and richly human; less like an animal, more like a god; less under the sway of irrational instincts, more truly a creature of rationality and responsible freedom.

37   WHERE THE WILD THYME BLOWS

"I know a bank whereon the wild thyme blows,
Where oxlips and the nodding violet grows
Quite over-canopied with luscious woodbine,
With sweet musk-roses, and with eglantine."
—WILLIAM SHAKESPEARE (1564-1616)

The winters are long in the north country where I live, and by March we are eager for spring. The sun climbs higher, yet winter tarries. We are, as Anne Allinson put it in *The Distaff*, "mired in monotony." But, wherever we live, there are times when our lives seem as dull as the weather without. The spirit's skies are cloudy, and the world presents a dreary face. Yet there is nothing inevitable about our moods. They vanish like ghosts when vigorously challenged. "My minde to me a kingdome is." In a moment, by mental legerdemain, I may leave the dirty slush of March and be at "a bank whereon the wild thyme blows." I know a point where the blue lupins march down to the sea; a forest glade where the dogwood blooms; a back road lined with goldenrod and fireweed, and quite overgrown with sweet wild roses.

Everyone has his favorite spots, his choicest memories. There is a lake at sunset, the pool where we like best to drop our fly. There is the smell of bacon and coffee on the campfire. The remembered thought of beauty is a magic wand. Our listlessness vanishes. We are out of our ruts, and away to the woods where we heard the thrush's cascading melody at dusk; or out under the stars, the night we watched Orion and Pleiades rise and climb and set, at last, as the eastern sky began to pale. We re-live these precious moments at will, and know how truly the poet spoke of:

> *"Those recollected hours that have the charm*
> *Of visionary things, those lovely forms*
> *And sweet sensations that throw back our life,*
> *And almost make remotest infancy*
> *A visible scene, on which the sun is shining . . ."*
>
> — WILLIAM WORDSWORTH (1770-1850)

38   CANST THOU BY SEARCHING FIND OUT GOD?

"I believe in God as I believe in my friends, because I feel the breath of His affection, feel His invisible and intangible hand drawing me, leading me, grasping me."

— MIGUEL DE UNAMUNO (1864-1936)

How well to be reminded that more basic than intellectual speculation about God is the experience of his reality. It is one thing to profess belief in God; another to "feel his invisible and intangible hand" — to be able to say, with the Psalmist: "Yea, though I walk through the valley of the shadow of death, thou art with me, thy rod and thy staff they comfort me."

This is to know God. But how do we attain such knowledge?

Well, how do I know my friends, how do I know myself? I know you because I see you, hear your voice, feel your handclasp. But as acquaintance ripens into friendship, there must be a sharing of thought and experience, an interweaving of the threads of our existence. At first, my knowledge rests upon the message my senses bring; but as my knowledge of you deepens, non-sensory factors develop — invisible lines of communication, unaffected by

51

distance, unsevered by death.

How do I know myself? I feel satisfaction or frustration, pleasure or pain. I am a physical organism and can see my image in the glass. But such sensory knowing is superficial. Self-knowing requires long searching, a stringent honesty. For there is within us a secret country, as unknown as Tibet. How do we enter there? By quiet thoughtfulness, by retiring from chatter and busy-ness and all bombardment of the senses. There are deeps within us, a realm of silence, and until we learn to penetrate there we cannot say, "I know myself."

We know God in much the same manner. In a limited way, we know him through sensory communication. The order and beauty of nature suggest a Creative Agent. Our minds may suggest God as "the most reasonable hypothesis." But true knowing comes neither by intellectual inquiry alone, nor through the senses alone. We know him as, in our privacy, we learn to attend to him, address our thoughts to him, wait patiently for him. With patience, with humility, we shall come in due time to "feel the breath of his affection." But we will not find him if we are forever avoiding him, if we keep filling our lives with sensory stimuli and a treadmill of activity. We will never find anybody that way — neither our friend, nor ourself, nor God.

"In many forms we try
To utter God's infinity
But the boundless hath no form,
And the Universal Friend
Doth as far transcend
An angel as a worm.

The great Idea baffles wit,
Language falters under it,
It leaves the learned in the lurch;
No art, nor power, nor toil can find
The measure of the eternal Mind,
Nor hymn, nor prayer, nor church."

— RALPH WALDO EMERSON (1803-82)

"Prayer is the serious, thoughtful, persistent endeavor to put our lives at the service of the best. It is the deliberate and systematic effort to develop inner resources adequate to meet life's demands."
— FREDERICK MAY ELIOT (1890-1958)

I acknowledge my need to grow quiet and composed, in order that I may become whole and live with clearer intention. Under the weight of daily pressures and many responsibilities, I have dissipated my powers and become fragmented. The results are not gratifying.

How often I have missed opportunities to help another person. I saw the need, but irresolution delayed me; or, preoccupied, I didn't see the need until it was too late.

How often I have been silent when I should have spoken forthrightly, timid when I should have been bold, critical when understanding and patience were called for, and hesitant when I should have acted with decision.

How often I have failed to foresee the consequences of my acts, and suffered from moral myopia; or, wearied by long hours of struggle, have I given way to despondency.

How often have I punished myself, not because of evil done, but out of some sense of my own unworthiness. I have indulged in morbid fancies of imaginary backslidings, I have lacked trust in my own productive capacities, and in my powers of reason and goodness.

So let me, in communion with the mysterious creative and constructive energies that forever surround and flow through me, cultivate the courage to be more faithful to my own best. Let me gain sounder knowledge of myself, my strengths and weaknesses, my good and my evil. Let me gain truer knowledge of others, also, in their likenesses to me and their differences from me, so that I may deal with their real selves, measuring their feelings by my own, yet patiently considering their varied lives and thoughts and circumstances. From false judgments, misplaced trust and distrust, misplaced giving and refusing, misplaced praise and rebuke, let me henceforth be successfully delivered.

From this quiet time, let me go forth afresh to meet the pressures and responsibilities of this day, ready to persevere through success and failure, through good report and evil report, affirming my faith in myself and in mankind, and celebrating my confidence in the goodness of life.

"The answer to our prayer may be the echo of our resolve."
— HERBERT LOUIS SAMUEL (1870-1963)

40 SERENITY, COURAGE, AND WISDOM

"Grant us the serenity of mind to accept that which cannot be changed, the courage to change that which can be changed, and the wisdom to tell one from the other."

—AUTHOR UNKNOWN
(frequently but erroneously attributed to REINHOLD NIEBUHR)

It is wisdom to accept serenely what we cannot change. Much worrying is wasted. "The beginning of wisdom," wrote Maeterlinck, "is the acknowledgment of our creaturehood." We humans are not gods, though we may try to play that role. We are mortal creatures, limited by time and space, ignorance and disease. We may to some degree be "the captains of our souls," but despite the poet by no stretch of the imagination can we really be the "masters of our fate." Human life is a fragile, contingent affair, here on this speck of star-dust where life became possible eons ago by an improbable series of lucky circumstances. Acknowledging our creaturehood means accepting many things we have no possibility of changing.

But it is not wisdom to accept what can and ought to be changed. Religion is not properly a search for happiness or for peace of mind, although the true saint is radiant and the man of faith is serene. But the radiance and the serenity are the fruits of righteousness; they are the by-products of meeting certain conditions. "There is only one way to be an ethical individual," said Josiah Royce, "and that is to choose your cause and then to serve it." There is far too much wrong with the world for any ethical person to be complacent. Not to be worried about the state of the nation and the ominous problems of mankind is to be morally derelict, religiously delinquent. We can never be satisfied with a serenity that is divorced from social concern, from a courageous willingness to wrestle with the important issues of our time; or divorced, for that matter, from a courageous effort to change in ourselves whatever needs changing.

As the prayer-sentence suggests, it takes the wisdom of Solomon to know the difference between what is truly unchangeable and inevitable, and what is not. If anything is apparent right now in the turmoil of our time, it is that many things our fathers thought were fixed and immutable, and that we, too, have so regarded, are now changing before our very eyes. War, racism, hunger, poverty, over-population, pollution: it is easy to submit to the notion that such giant ills are indeed insoluble. But heaven help us, if they are; this would mean that the human experiment is fast approaching a dead end.

The Apostle Paul also lived in a turbulent time. He knew what it was to be ridiculed, mobbed, beaten; his ministry was a saga filled with hardship, ending with imprisonment and probably execution. Yet he wrote of "the peace that passes all understanding," and described his ministry as: "This priceless treasure we hold, so to speak, in a common earthenware jar . . . We are handicapped on all sides but we are never frustrated; we are puzzled, but never in despair. We are persecuted, but never have to stand it alone; we are knocked down but we are never knocked out . . . always 'going through it' yet never 'going under' . . . We are penniless, and yet in reality we have everything worth having."

With such courage, such faith, a man is not invulnerable since vulnerability is of the nature of creaturehood. But he can know a serenity of mind that accepts the limitations and uncertainty of this mortal state. He can labor to change what needs changing; he knows, indeed, that he is not free to desist from such labor. Yet remembering he is a creature of a brief hour, he can also know that he is not required to perform the Atlas feat of shouldering God's entire burden himself.

Real religion is no rule of safety; it is an adventure. There are no spiritual short-cuts, no religious "miracle drugs." Serenity of mind comes not by seeking it through nostrums, but by finding a cause to work for, a God to serve, a God who summons us to ethical responsibility, to love of enemies, to great-hearted compassion, to respect for persons. In the service of such a God, I have little doubt, we shall win through at last to "the peace that passes all understanding."

41   WHERE TWO OR THREE ARE GATHERED

"Do you together walk, together hold converse, together come to a common mind, even as they who walked before us, finding knowledge together, worshipped as one."

          —THE RIG-VEDA (The Second Millenium B.C.)

Reacting from churchgoing as a duty, many of us swing to the opposite extreme, underestimating the value of communal worship. "I can worship better in my garden," we say. "Isn't God everywhere? What need have I of a special place and time?" Of course we can worship anywhere. If worship means very much to us, we shall worship many times between each weekly visit to the kirk. But what can be done anytime easily becomes what is seldom done at all. The neglect of communal worship generally means the decline of private worship.

Further, religion is never simply a matter of a person's relationship to God; to be in any sense well rounded, it must involve his relations with his fellows. The verse, "He that loveth not his brother whom he hath seen, how can he love God whom he hath not seen?" contains a profound insight (*I John* 4:20). The same is true of the words, "Where two or three are gathered together in my name, there am I in the midst of them" (*Matthew* 18:20). It has been said that religion is what a man does with his own solitariness — again, a profound insight. But equally true is it to say that religion is what men do with their togetherness.

The ancient Indian scripture holds wisdom for us. What this old world needs desperately is for men to walk together, talk together, and come to a common mind. Having achieved brotherhood, shall they not have less difficulty finding him whom the Nazarene called "Father?"

"Let us choose therefore to commune where there is the warmest sense of religion, where devotion exceeds formality, and practice must correspond with profession and where there is at least as much charity as zeal."

          — WILLIAM PENN (1644-1718)

"A man should utter daily a hundred benedictions."

—RABBI MEIR (2nd Century, A.D.)

Providence: what an old-fashioned word! Like "grace." But how bountifully nature provides, nourishing our bodies, feeding our spirits. Men have long imagined that rare foresight must have been used to anticipate their every need. We speak of the necessities of life. They are really very few — air, water, food, sunlight. We ought also to think of life's surpluses, all of life's gratuitous gifts. Take water. Indispensible, of course, and utilitarian. Without it our earth would be barren as the moon. And we ourselves are ninety-some percent water, and must replenish our supply regularly. But water is so much more than H_2O. Catch snowflakes on black velvet. Look in the western sky at sunset. From the bubbling spring deep in the forest, among moss-covered rocks, to the mighty roar of Niagara's cataract; from the dew on the meadow to the high-flung spray on the rocky shore; from the gentle patter of rain on the roof to the frenzied white-caps during a sudden storm — endless in variety, in loveliness, is water.

The loveliness of the earth, the magic of changing seasons, the richness of foliage, the music of bird-song, the iridescence of butterfly wing, the grandeur of snowcapped peak — what a world, that should drive us to Emerson's conclusion:

"I do not so much wonder at a snowflake, a shell, a summer landscape, or the glory of the stars; but at the necessity of beauty under which the universe lies."

All this, and a great deal more, the word "providence" endeavors to embrace, the rich providing of nature. In fact, if there be reason to doubt nature's impartiality, must it not be because we fare so much better than we deserve, and receive from life far more than we can possibly return. Cause and effect, yes, and strict impartiality, such is our world, so far as we can see. God does not play favorites. Yet the divine law seems to return a generous bonus. Life's goodness, like a parent's love, comes beyond our power to earn it.

Should we not, as the ancient Rabbi said, "utter daily a hundred benedictions?"

"Though our mouths were full of song as the sea, and our tongues of exultation as the multitude of its waves, and our lips of praise as the wide-extended firmament; though our eyes shone with light like the sun and the moon, and our hands were spread forth like the eagles of heaven, and our feet were swift as hinds, we should still be unable to thank thee and to bless thy name, O Lord our God and God of our fathers, for one thousandth or one ten thousandth part of the bounties which thou has bestowed upon our fathers and upon us."

— THE HEBREW MORNING SERVICE

43 STILL AND COOL

"Be still and cool in thy own mind and spirit."

— GEORGE FOX (1624-91)

Only when the lake is calm can it mirror the sky. Wind-ruffled, the sky's reflection is shattered. Even so, only by calling the heart home to quiet, only by stilling the restless surface and sinking down into the undisturbed, tranquil depths of our being, can we restore the divine image and perceive the wholeness, the holiness of our being. Therefore, addressing myself, I say:

Relax; let go all accumulated tensions of your body. Perfect relaxation is an art to be patiently learned. It cannot be achieved by effort. You have to stop trying.

More difficult than relaxing the body, however, is quieting the mind. You must silence the racing thoughts, lay aside your cares, and repeatedly usher out whatever mental images flit across your internal screen. Listen to the "voice" you have been drowning out. Be receptive to creative insights; learn what, given a chance, will rise to the surface.

Mastering the art of growing quiet and receptive to whatever the silence has to teach opens the way to growth and renewal. One rises imperceptably but surely, like a ship in a lock. Gradually much that has seemed important becomes inconsequential. In the stillness, and as if in the presence of one who is truth and love, let your true priorities emerge. See what it is you truly want: not these trivial baubles, these glittering fancies you have chased so hard, but something else. Men call it different names, or leave it nameless; but the heart knows it by one thing. Buddha called it Nirvana, enlightenment; Laotse called it Tao, the way; Paul, the peace that passes understanding.

The word now is patience, and persistence. You cannot hasten this process. You must wait. Your part is your willingness — your willingness to hear the inner voice, to stand before the inner judge defenceless. Be still; wait. Do not be anxious for quick results, or concerned about what you will bring back from this pilgrimage of the spirit. You may not know. You may think nothing. But it will not be nothing, only something different than you expect. In the deeper sense, you are not trying to get anything, only to be. You seek only to be yourself, to gain the true quality of your being.

Do not be afraid. Do not fight the silence, or fear failure in this venture. Give yourself to these moments. Let the results be what they will. "Be still and cool in thy own mind and spirit." Be still and know that that which you seek is not far away. It is here — or He is here. And you are His. And nothing can separate you from His love.

44 THE POISON OF HATE

"Love ye, therefore, one another from the heart; and if a man sin against thee, cast forth the poison of hate and speak peaceably to him, and in thy soul hold not guile; and if he confess and repent, forgive him."
—THE APOCRYPHAL TESTAMENT OF GAD (6:3)

Whether these words were actually spoken by Jesus we cannot say; it is not probable. But they convey his spirit as surely as did the Apostle Paul in the twelfth chapter of *Romans*. We like the emphasis that hatred is a poison, and that the abused needs to forgive as badly as the abuser needs forgiveness. Whatever bitterness and resentment we allow to build up within us, whatever the justification, acts to our own detriment. The intertwining relationship of psyche and soma, of our emotional and physical health, is nowhere more clearly apparent. Active hate produces measurable physiological effects, contracting the arteries, overloading the heart. Smoldering resentments and an embittered outlook on life produce deleterious chemical reactions. Love, likewise, produces measurable change, but beneficial to the organism; good cheer and laughter are "the medicine of life." With ill will in our hearts we move toward sickness, with good will toward health.

We need to forgive. Jesus strongly emphasized unlimited readiness to forgive — not "seven times, but seventy times seven," or without limit. And where forgiveness is impossible or inappropriate, hatred, bitterness, a retaliatory attitude must be rejected. Forgiveness properly waits upon the wrongdoer's confession and repentance, his desire to be forgiven. To forgive one who persists in wrongdoing may be an unethical condoning of evil. But where we cannot forgive, we must hold ourselves *ready* to forgive, and, by speaking peaceably, seek to dissuade the wrongdoer.

" 'When a man sees that his neighbor hates him,' said Rabbi Rafael of Berschad, 'then he must love him more than he did before to fill up what is lacking . . .' Rabbi Rafael used always to warn against applying the measuring-rod in one's dealings with people: A surplus of love is necessary to fill up what is lacking of love in this world."

—MARTIN BUBER (1878-1965)

45 THIS ALTERNATION OF VISION AND BLINDNESS

"One does not doubt the existence of air because a strong wind is not always blowing, or of sunlight because night intervenes between dawn and dusk."

— SRI AUROBINDO (1872-1950)

In the hour of solitude, yet also sometimes in the noisy bustle of the city's traffic; in the rare ecstatic moment when the bush flames and all is transfigured, but also in the commonplace miracle of each new sunrise, each evening's sunset glory; in the still, small voice, but also in the prophet's denunciation, thou makest thyself known to thy doubting, would-be believing children. Whenever, wherever, however thou makest thyself known to us, may we have grace to hear and understand. And if we catch nothing but the eternal silence and no flicker of divine light breaks through the opaqueness of our spirits, grant us patience, let us persevere.

Often, we suppose, thou has spoken to us, not in words sounding but in the wordless languages of beauty and love and justice, and the message has fallen on rocky soil where it could not sprout; or on shallow soil where it found no lasting rootage. Often we have glimpsed thy truth, caught a fleeting vision of thy glory, and our hearts rejoiced; but the vision faded, darkness followed day, and now we wonder whether it was but an illusion, a mirage.

In this alternation of vision and blindness, of belief and doubt, of growing wisdom and of spiritual lethargy, may we recognize a universal human experience. All men have found, even the most saintly, times of spiritual drought and darkness. Every serious seeker discovers how essential it is to push forward in storm as in sunshine, guided by whatever stars are shining. Or, if even the stars are clouded, trudging on in faith, hoping and looking for the dawning, and clinging to love as the touchstone, the ultimate secret of life.

O Perfect Love, whenever we submit to thee, thou turnest us to works of mercy and neighborliness, to be mediators of thy love. So, even when we cannot find thee, still turn us to our brothers, to bind up the wounded, to heal the broken-hearted, and to set at liberty those who are oppressed.

"There is that near thee that will guide thee. O wait for it and be sure that thee keep it."

— ISAAC PENNINGTON (1617-80)

46 BREAD AND HUNGER

"Give bread to those who have hunger, and hunger to those who have bread."

— AN OLD PRAYER

It is an appalling fact with which all of us well-fed, well-sheltered Americans must live: that we, who so seldom experience physical want and who know hunger only as a healthy appetite, must live in a world where ten thousand people die of hunger every day, a world of steadily growing hunger, as food production fails to increase as rapidly as mankind's imploding population. What can an ethical person do with an inescapable, unthinkable fact like this, that half the world's children suffer malnutrition, while we eat like ancient Rome's elite, or a good deal better?

No easy answer suggests itself. We can, of course, do something, make small practical gestures; indeed we must, if we are to preserve any moral sensitivity. The giant proportions of the problem do not invalidate our small personal efforts, both political and philanthropic. Still, the mountain of human misery remains despite our removal of a grain or two of sand. Not even a sacrificial tithe can alleviate the weight of our concern. Nor will some manipulative God answer us if we pray, "Give bread to those who have hunger." The fertility of the earth is already given, the knowledge necessary to curb unwanted births and starvation is already found. The task, therefore, is man's, not God's.

Precisely for this reason, because the task is ours, must we pray, "Give bread to those who have hunger, and hunger to those who have bread" — this, or its equivalent. For we who have ample bread must bring ourselves to know hunger, the spiritual hunger that Jesus called blessed, the hunger for righteousness, the passionate concern for justice and the compassion that identifies with the wretched of the earth. And in the privacy of our own thoughts, must we not insist on learning whether we can really cultivate such spiritual hunger, such passion and compassion, unless we radically amend our values, the values of our military-industrial, affluent society? If we really mean, "Give bread to those who have hunger," it is our bread and their hunger that we will have to share. It is our lives as well as theirs that must be changed.

"Alas for you who are rich; you have had your time of happiness. Alas for you who are well-fed now; you shall go hungry."

— LUKE 6:24-25

"Feed the man dying of hunger, because if you have not fed him, you have killed him."

— AN ANCIENT CHURCH FATHER

"Do not accept what you hear by report, do not accept tradition, do not accept a statement because it is found in our books . . . nor because it is the saying of your teacher . . . But be ye lamps unto yourselves; be your own confidence; hold to the truth within yourselves."

— GAUTAMA (c. 500 B.C.)

According to tradition, a man once asked Gautama, "Are you a god?" "No," he replied. "An angel?" "No." "A saint?" "No." "Then what are you?" And he answered, "I am awake." And this became his name, Buddha, the awakened one, the enlightened.

Really to be awakened seems to have been the heart of the original Buddhist message — to be aware, really to break out of the paralyzing cocoon of egocentricity. Buddhism, Lin Yutang once wrote, "began with a ringing call to energy and sought to stab men awake."

This is a different picture than most westerners have of this great eastern religion. Schweitzer called it "world-denying" and hopelessly pessimistic; Santayana said that "Buddhism tried to quiet a sick world with anaesthetics, while Christianity sought to purge it with fire."

Whatever Buddhism has been through the centuries, there is little reason to doubt that such judgments are grossly unfair if applied to its founder. Gautama, one of the greatest men ever to live, was a man of unbounded energy who trudged the dusty roads of India for nearly half a century, calling men to live an examined life. He labored diligently to reform the Hinduism into which he had been born, which he saw as decadent, idolatrous, and thoroughly externalized into elaborate rituals. Like Gandhi, however, he knew that the life of action must be balanced and renewed by regular periods of withdrawal and meditation. Three times each day he reserved a period of quiet, that, as Huston Smith puts it, "through meditation he might restore his center of gravity to its sacred inner pivot." And each year, during the rainy season, he suspended his busy schedule of teaching and preaching, to retire with his monks in retreat for three months.

Gautama does not deserve to be called pessimistic. True, he stressed that life is filled with sorrow. Man is finite, life is transitory. Sickness, old age, bereavement, death — who can ever escape these? But Gautama was fundamentally optimistic, for he said: "One thing I teach: suffering *and the end of suffering.*" Suffering can be overcome; not easily, but only when we set ourselves free from what, being mortal, we cannot have or cannot keep. The answer is as simple, and as difficult as this: man must transcend himself, and his unrealistic and selfish cravings. By conquest of egotism, by faithful adherence to the Eightfold Path, one can hope ultimately to achieve liberation, serenity, insight into truth, love for all creation and all creatures, and the deep joy of union with reality.

How close to the Sermon on the Mount are Gautama's words: "Let a man overcome anger by love; let him overcome evil by good; let him overcome the greedy by liberality, the liar by truth."

Divested of the legendary and miraculous elements in which a credulous, magic-loving world clothed him, Gautama emerges as a person of rich warmth and vigor and wisdom, a man of deep compassion and empathy, of profound psychological insights. This fully awakened one can still remind us that noble religion need not be theistic or speculative; that human nature can be changed, even though to change it requires hard work; and that a man can awaken himself, with perseverence, self-discipline, and patient practice of the art of meditation.

May something of the spirit of the Lord Buddha come to us, something of his tranquility of mind, through patient seeking and quiet hours of thought. And may there flow from us to all mankind something of his compassionate spirit.

May we awaken from illusion and falsehood, and shake off the shackles of egoism. And may we grow in self-mastery, and strive for maturity.

So may God be spirit within us, and spirit from us, helping to knit the world into brotherly unity.

48   THE INWARD JOURNEY: I

"In the middle of the journey of our life I came to myself in a dark wood where the straight way was lost . . . I cannot rightly tell how I entered it, so full of sleep was I about the moment that I left the

— DANTE ALIGHIERI (1265-1321)

Through the ages the idea of pilgrimage has been common. The devout Moslem still hopes to make his pilgrimage to Mecca before he dies. Christians and Jews have made theirs to the Holy Land; Catholics to Rome, and a thousand lesser shrines. According to Chaucer, it was in the month of April, when "sweet showers fall," that he met a group of pilgrims at the Tabard Inn in Southwark, all on their way to the shrine of St. Thomas a Becket, the most famous of English martyrs, murdered in the Cathedral in Canterbury in 1170. For hundreds of years, many such pilgrims came to Canterbury from "every shire's end" in England.

But "going on pilgrimage" is really only an external acting out of what, to have real significance, must be an inward journey. The Arthurian legends of the search for the Holy Grail may be read as tales of adventure; they are also to be read as allegories that give an account of man's subjective experiences, projected by means of vivid imagery. The dragons, evil knights, and enchanted maidens are not simply fictional inventions. They stand for elements deep in the human psyche, for the strange, hidden forces we moderns call "the Unconscious."

While Dante undoubtedly believed in the three-storied universe, to read his allegory simply as an attempt to give a literal description of Hell, Purgatory, and Heaven is to miss the point rather badly. Dante was a superlative story teller; but the lasting significance of *The Divine Comedy* lies in his description of that unconscious world within us all where an inner drama is proceeding — a drama of which ordinarily we are largely if not entirely unaware. True, Dante would not have thought of it just this way; at least he would not have used Freudian or Jungian terms. But it has long been recognized that *The Divine Comedy* has no less than three levels of meaning: the literal story of the poet's pilgrimage into the afterworld; but also, a telling political satire. The third level, for us by far the most important, is its allegorical representation of an exploration of the deeper levels of the psyche, a strange and difficult yet ultimately rewarding journey wherein the individual learns to recognize in himself the need to be reunited with all that he has repressed and driven out of consciousness. It is on this deeper level of meaning that this medieval Italian masterpiece remains well worth studying. So read, it can serve the modern pilgrim, as it has served many earlier generations of seekers.

"I sent my soul through the invisible
Some letter of that after-life to spell.
And by and by my soul returned to me,
And answered, 'I myself am heaven and hell.' "

—OMAR KHAYYÁM (d. 1123?)

49   THE INWARD JOURNEY: II

"As I walked through the wilderness of this life, I lighted on a certain place where was a den, and I laid me down in that place to sleep, and as I slept I dreamed a dream."

— JOHN BUNYAN (1628-88)

So opens "one of the most astonishing miracles of literary history," John Bunyan's *Pilgrim's Progress.* For three hundred years many persons have placed it next to their Bibles, treasuring this timeless account of the soul's struggle to win self-mastery, wholeness, and self-knowledge; or, to use Jung's term: "individuation." The Puritan theology of this nearly illiterate mender of pots and pans is a far cry from ours today; such strict Calvinsim has little appeal for us. As literature a better case can be made. This little-educated man wrote with a refreshing directness. His thorough familiarity with the Bible stood him in good stead. But our interest stems from the allegorical nature of this classic.

Bunyan's hero, Christian, is Everyman. And every man has the choice whether or not to be a "pilgrim." Shall we resolutely put behind us the City of Destruction, and set out across the Slough of Despond towards the wicket gate? Or shall we settle down to compromise and comfort, to the life of thoughtless respectability, of safety, security, and mediocrity? If we decide to undertake the spiritual or psychological ardors of pilgrimage, we shall no doubt meet adventures similar to those Bunyan described, even the chained lion guarding the path to the House Beautiful, and the fearsome monster, Appolyon, and Giant Despair. But, hopefully, the meaning of our life will begin to unfold itself a little more clearly. We shall with good fortune cross the Valley of the Shadow of Death and come at last to the Delectable Mountains and

Country of Beulah. What Bunyan called Salvation, we may prefer to call wholeness or fulfillment of the self. No matter, what matters is seeing that Christian's difficulties are simply projections of the problems that Everyman finds within himself — finds if he looks, or fails to recognize if he does not. Whoever would escape the City of Destruction, or successfully by-pass Vanity Fair must gird his loins for strenuous effort. As Froude said: "Man's spiritual existence is like the flight of a bird in the air . . . When man ceases to exert himself he falls."

Christian meets Obstinate and Pliable. We also harbor these characters — our obstinate self-will and our persisting core of infantilism. Christian succeeds in resisting their persuasions, only to be assailed by other temptations. Mr. Worldly-wiseman nearly succeeds in luring him into abandoning this journey. Soon thereafter Formalist and Hypocrisy come tumbling over the wall and try to convince him of the rightness of their way. Later, when he attempts to arouse Sloth and Presumption, he self-righteously assumes he will never be guilty of these particular weaknesses. But shortly thereafter he falls asleep in the arbor and loses the scroll that has been provided to guide him. So it goes through the whole narrative. And so indeed does it go on the inward journey. We think we have conquered some weakness, and then are more subtly beset by the same temptation, usually in a most innocent-appearing guise. It takes many small victories to win this war.

A thoughtful reading can provide us with numerous insights for the journey of the soul towards wholeness. It can help us understand how many of the problems we face are not "out there" in other people, or in circumstances beyond our control, but are in fact in ourselves; and their solution requires nothing less than a fundamental change in us, in our attitudes, in our own psyche.

When we have pondered why Christian, as he climbed the Hill Difficulty, midway lost his heavy burden, it may occur to us that we, too, have begun our pilgrimage of the spirit for inadequate reasons; have begun it hoping to be rid of certain uncomfortable symptoms. This recognized, we now are ready to go on with a more positive objective; not to be rid of symptoms, but to attain wholeness and fullness of being.

To persist in this journey is no easy thing. Like Christian, we shall meet temptations to give up under many guises. He is repeatedly tempted, and betrayed, by the tendency to fall asleep.

So it is with us. Sloth is one great enemy of the spiritual life: to take the easy way, which alas we learn eventually does not take us where we want to go. Mr. Wordly-wiseman represents another temptation. He tries to persuade Christian to turn aside and settle down in a town called Morality, where lives a gentleman named Legality, highly skilled in helping men off with such burdens as Christian's. It is common to think of morality as a matter of obeying rules and observing customs; thus, it is thought, can one ease one's conscience of its burden of guilt. Settle down in Morality Town, live a "normal life," and forget the impossible dream, the unreachable goal.

"When will men learn," wrote Samuel M. Crothers, whose second New Testament was *Pilgrim's Progress,* "that morality is not a town, but a road, and that the truly moral thing is to keep moving."

To keep moving, to keep on growing: this is the great requirement of life — that we be seekers, pilgrims, striving to be fully ourselves, to become fully ourselves, to reach our spiritual potential.

"Then said Evangelist, pointing with his finger over a very wide field, 'Do you see yonder wicket gate?' The man said 'No.' Then said the other, 'Do you see yonder shining light?' He said, 'I think I do.' Then said Evangelist, 'Keep that light in thine eyes, and go up directly thereto.' "

— JOHN BUNYAN

50   TONS OF DISCIPLINE

"Thank God every morning when you get up that you have something to do that day which must be done, whether you like it or not."

— CHARLES KINGSLEY (1819-75)

Robert Frost in his later years was not adverse to giving young writers wise counsel, and I have not forgotten his saying that "life is tons of discipline." The writer knows this as well as anyone, and the serious poet best of all. But self-discipline is a main key to success in any occupation. It is an essential ingredient in the art of living. Will power may be an old-fashioned sounding virtue, but there is really no avoiding it if we are in earnest about life.

There are many things we have to do in life, whoever we are, however we make our living — things we have to do, whether we want to or not. And curiously, the fact that this is so is no cause for unhappiness. Happiness doesn't derive nearly so much from being able to do just what we want, as from having something useful, even demanding and challenging, that we have to do.

"Happy is he who has learned this one thing: to do the plain duty of the moment quickly and cheerfully, whatever it may be."

Such homely advice may sound antiquated, but one wonders how much contemporary unhappiness is rooted in the opposite philosophy that dismisses duty and wants all life to be fun and games.

"Blessed is he who carries within himself a God, an ideal, and who obeys it — ideal of art, ideal of science, ideal of gospel virtues: therein lie the springs of great thoughts and great actions; they all reflect light from the Infinite."

— LOUIS PASTEUR (1822-95)

51 WILLING TO PRAY, READY TO PRAISE

"Prayer is the very soul and essence of religion. Therefore prayer must be the very core of the life of man; for no man can live without religion."

—MOHANDAS K. GANDHI (1869-1948)

Let us be willing to pray. Every man has much to pray for. We stand in need of wisdom, of courage, of patience, of insight, of forgiveness, of faith. So let there be prayer in our hearts; the prayer that is longing for righteousness, the prayer that is acknowledgment of shortcoming, the prayer that is resolve, and quiet self-determination, and a rich wanting for greater wisdom and a greater lovingness.

Let us be ready to give praise — praise that is joy, praise that is acceptance, praise that is adoration and gratitude both for what has been given — and what has been withheld.

Let us not be afraid to offer once again our allegiance and pray that God may so capture our devotion that we may worship him not with pious words only, but with honest, self-disciplined, and loving lives.

"To meditate daily, to pray daily, seems a means indispensable for breaking this surface crust of formality, habit, routine, which hides the living spring of wisdom."
— ORVILLE DEWEY (1794-1882)

52 FINDING AND LOSING YOURSELF

"The true value of a human being is determined primarily by the measure and the sense in which he has attained liberation from the self."
— ALBERT EINSTEIN (1879-1955)

Throughout this collection of thoughts, we have stressed the importance of seeking a fuller knowledge of oneself. It is curious that we should ever feel this need to know ourselves, or to find ourselves. What is closer to a person than himself? What is seemingly more accessible? But since antiquity men have sensed that the self is an ocean whose depths lie hidden. We see the surface, we explore the shallows. But the ocean of self has boundaries we can never reach, depths we can never plumb.

"To be nobody-but-myself," wrote e. e. Cumings, "in a world which is doing its best, night and day, to make me everybody else, means the hardest battle which any man can fight, and never stop fighting." It has often seemed to thoughtful men that society is a vast, if unorganized conspiracy to make us like everyone else. But finding oneself is not simply a battle against external pressures to conform. This self we seek is not a simple nor static entity. It is a river, growing and developing, or perhaps shrinking and drying up, but in any case a changing reality. What we are seeking is also something we are creating. Each day life introduces us to country we have yet to explore, to experiences different than we have known. Day by day, therefore, we are becoming a different person, however slight the difference. So finding out about ourselves is a never-finished adventure.

The task is made more difficult because modern life inundates us with machines, gadgets, labor-savers; our minds are flooded with news and information from the media. We read of "the molders of public opinion" without stopping to realize it is we whom the molders seek to mold. Advertisers try to make us want what they are paid to make sell. Even the banks urge us to mortgage our future to them, to take that Carribean vacation now, and pay for it later. We go along, more or less, taking the line of least resistance. The sober truth is that it is hard to live an authentic, autonomous life under any circumstances. Modern life only makes it tougher. Intentional living requires the courage to face the truth about ourselves, as well as persistence, leisure, room for revery, and space — what the Overstreets call "psychic space."

"There is no greater curse," said Laotse, "than lack of contentment, no greater sin than the desire for possession . . . Which is the greater evil — loss of self, or of possessions?"

Such words foreshadow those of Jesus: "He who finds his life will lose it, and he who loses his life for my sake will find it." This paradox suggests that if a man wants to find his true self, he must do more than successfully ward off the pressures of society to conform. He must also escape entanglement in his own ego. He must find something larger than himself, a cause in which he can invest himself, body and soul. Only a commanding loyalty can free a person from imprisoning self-concern and self preoccupation. But this losing oneself is the truest sort of finding. It is discovering that living is an exciting enterprise, and most rewarding when it is lived as much for others as for oneself.

Every man must make his choice. If he chooses to live for self, without commanding loyalties, he will never really find himself, nor be able to draw from the hidden depths of his being the sort of self he is capable of becoming. If he chooses the way of commitment, dedicating himself to the noblest purposes he can find, making his real vocation a life of strenuous moral effort, honest thinking, and generous service, in thus "losing" himself he will truly find.

53 THE ROAD TO MANHOOD

"Man is not Man as yet."

—ROBERT BROWNING (1812-89)

It sounds like a play on words. Actually, the Victorian poet was reflecting the optimism of his day, that found rich grounds for hope in the story of evolution. From the cooling oceans life had arisen, through millenia of millenia developing ever higher forms, until at last from simian ancestry emerged our earliest recognizable forebear. This first man, if we can call him that, was an ape-like predator, a killer who survived in the unceasing struggle for existence by his cunning. He was human, but only in the primitive sense of having discovered that the thigh-bone of an antelope made an excellent skull-crusher, a weapon equally effective in securing game or eliminating a rival.

Browning thought that our race had come a long way since our "African genesis," as, of course, in many ways it has. With exuberant confidence few of us still possess, he believed that "progress is the law of life."

What optimism we can summon is of a more tempered sort. We at least see Man as a species still becoming, not yet arrived. Our "reach exceeds our grasp." Our potentialities are not fulfilled. We begin to understand that ingenuity — bigger and better weapons — cannot save us. Our killer instinct must be successfully brought under control; our strong aggressive drive that once served our species well must now be tamed, redirected, and harnessed to socially constructive ends. But how can this be achieved, at least in the time homo sapiens is likely to have in its race with catastrophe? Is Man reaching the point in his evolution where he can consciously assist and hasten the process? We can only hope so. It's a matter of faith rather than knowledge. As individuals, none of us will know the outcome of the human venture; we will all be long gone.

Since we cannot read the future, and only to a limited degree can make it our concern, each of us has this more immediate task, this prime responsibility: To evolve as an individual member of our species into a person as fully human, as richly self-fulfilled, as creatively and constructively outgoing, as it is possible for us to become. Each of us must resolve to become a person who, if there were enough such, would assure the future of mankind.

For what is the wisdom the race needs in order to survive? We can give it various names: co-operation, mutuality, reciprocity, charity, compassion, the ability to live in peace with fellowman — all this, and more. The truth is, we have no one word adequate to connote the full dimension of this wisdom, this taming and civilizing of our instinctual heritage. We find something of this wisdom memorably expressed in the prayer attributed to the

72

gentle saint of Assisi:

"Grant that I may not so much seek to be comforted as to comfort; to be understood, as to understand; to be loved as to love; for it is in giving that we receive."
—FRANCIS OF ASSISI (1182-1226)

54 THE MINISTRY OF ART

"There is no surer way of evading the world than through art."
—JOHANN WOLFGANG VON GOETHE (1749-1832)

This is a sure insight. Beauty can tempt us away from moral obligations. A. Powell Davies once said that he found in his love of nature his greatest temptation. Like nature, art often is a way of escape, of avoiding responsible concern for the tragedies and agonies of our society. But if Goethe had stopped there, he would only have voiced a half-truth — the lesser half. However he continued: "And there is no surer way of binding oneself to the world than through art." Rightly regarded, art need not be a way of evading life, but of more successfully invading it. It does not ask us to turn our backs but to open our eyes.

A small replica of a beautiful statue has served many as an avenue to successful contemplation. What an orthodox Christian may discover in a crucifix, the religious liberal may more likely find in a work not so intimately associated with unacceptable dogma. We think of one friend who regularly communes with a copy of a seated Bodhisattva, the original carved in China many centuries ago. He finds it easier to practice quiet sitting before such a master of this art. Its gracious lines and harmonious curves speak to him of a life very different from his own. Without being a Buddhist, he has found profit in silent companionship with this Buddhist saint who, by long self-discipline and meditation, won through to liberation and serenity, but who, having qualified for Nirvana, voluntarily postponed his entry into this state of bliss in order to help his suffering fellow men.

Rilke in his poem, "Archaic Torso of an Apollo," wrote: "There is no part of it that does not see you. You must change your life."

Great art has a judgmental quality. A bronze Bodhisattva does not literally see us at all; but it can help us to see ourselves. We can

73

hear its "you must change your life." It rebukes us, exposes our thoughtless choices, our mediocrity, our self-deception. But sculpture will not speak to us unless we let it, wait for it. Like all forms of art, it requires our full concentration, and the courtesy of a leisurely attention and sustained exposure. As the old Chinese proverb puts it: "Approach a great painting as you would a great prince."

We talk much of self-knowledge, but often forget that self-knowledge is not acquired in a vacuum. We can learn about ourselves through our relationships with others; we can gain it through communion with nature. But one avenue we are wise not to neglect is the ministry of art.

"You use a glass mirror to see your face; you use works of art to see your soul."

—GEORGE BERNARD SHAW (1856-1950)

55   IN NO STRANGE LAND

"O world invisible, we view thee,
O world intangible, we touch thee,
O world unknowable, we know thee,
Inapprehensible, we clutch thee.

Does the fish soar to find the ocean,
The eagle plunge to find the air —
That we should ask the stars in motion
If they have rumor of thee there?

Not where the wheeling systems darken,
And our benumbed conceiving soars —
The drift of pinions, would we hearken,
Beats at our own clay-shuttered doors.

The angels keep their ancient places:
Turn but a stone, and start a wing!
'Tis ye, 'tis your estrangèd faces,
That miss the many-splendored thing."

—FRANCIS THOMPSON (1859-1907)

I came upon these verses by the Roman Catholic poet long ago, responded to them and memorized them. Only much later did I learn that this was an unpublished poem, found among Thompson's papers after his death. Only then did I discover that two final stanzas complete the message:

"But, when so sad thou canst not sadder,
Cry; — and upon thy so sore loss
Shall shine the traffic of Jacob's ladder
Pitched betwixt Heaven and Charing Cross.

Yea, in the night, my Soul, my daughter,
Cry, — clinging Heaven by the hems;
And lo, Christ walking on the water
Not of Gennesareth, but Thames!"

The penniless poet was a failure at everything save writing poetry. He slept many a night on the Thames Embankment. Long addicted to laudanum, an opium derivative, he was literally saved by the charity of a London prostitute who found him hungry and gave him food, sick and ministered unto him. Later, his literary genius was likewise rescued, this time by the poet, Alice Meynell, and her husband, Wilfred, who got him off the street and off of drugs, and his poetry into print. His "The Hound of Heaven" has been called one of the very few "great" odes the language can boast. It is quite possibly the most widely loved religious poem of this century.

"In No Strange Land" is a lesser achievement, but the imagery is memorable. We like the idea of Jacob's Ladder ascending from sooty, noisy old Charing Cross. Equally, we like the thought of the penniless drug addict "seeing" Christ walking on the River Thames. It is important to know that sacred reality (as Sir Julian Huxley calls it, wishing to avoid the word "God") is to be found not only where all is lovely and peaceful; that, like the sun, love shines everywhere. Whoever looks for divinity had best not overlook "the haunts of wretchedness and need, (the) shadowed thresholds dark with fears." God is to be sought by including the excluded, by befriending the lonely, by turning strangers into neighbors, and by finding avenues of usefulness and self-respect for the superannuated. He is to be found by gaining insight into the despair of the impotent, and understanding of the angry venom of those whom society's injustice has goaded into a hopeless, irrational espousal of violence. He is brought near when we demand equality before the law for all persons, when we labor to tame our urban jungles and tear down the invisible walls of our ghettos.

When a man turns his back on the misery and bafflement of his fellows, when he walls himself away in his private garden of comfort and respectability, others *may* be the losers, but he most surely is. True peace of mind involves finding our brothers, knowing that all men share our dreams and weep the same salt tears; and share the same fragile gift of life, the same glory, the same grief in being human.

> *"We do pray for mercy,*
> *And that same prayer doth teach us all to render*
> *The deeds of mercy."*

—WILLIAM SHAKESPEARE (1564-1616)

56 THANKS TO THE HUMAN HEART

> *"This prospect vast, what is it? — weighed aright,*
> *'Tis nature's system of divinity,*
> *And every student of the night inspires.*
> *'Tis elder scripture, writ by God's own hand . . .*
> *. . . . How great,*
> *How glorious, then, appears the mind of man,*
> *When in it all the stars and planets roll."*

—EDWARD YOUNG (1683-1765)

Far vaster than our fathers dreamed, this universe of a million billion galaxies. The vistas of immensity that staggered them keep growing, until our imaginations can be stretched no further. The questions with which they wrestled we come no nearer answering. Life for us as for them is bittersweet, its pleasures transient, its good fortunes subject to sudden reversal, its contentment always threatened by inexplicable tragedies. The more we love, the sharper are the pangs of sorrow in bereavement. The more sensitive and compassionate we let ourselves become, the greater the price life extracts. Surrounded by mystery, satiated with "miracles," we discover ourselves to be the greatest miracle of all, we in whose minds "the stars and planets roll," we who reach out for understanding, cherish values, and nurse great hopes.

This is wisdom: To walk with courage over the hills and valleys of our days, guided by the little we know and by our intuition of an overarching beneficent purpose; to make faith in life our polestar, trusting in the goodness of being; to remind ourselves daily, hourly, minute by minute, of all that we receive without our earning or deserving; to keep in loving remembrance the persons who bless our days and magnify our experience.

This, too, is wisdom: To regard self-pity as a cardinal vice, complaint and ingratitude as a betrayal of our trust; to withstand temptation and tribulation; to remain undaunted by dangers, unconquered by adversities, and untainted by cowardice.

And this is wisdom: To exchange our selfish pre-occupation for a cheerful outgoingness; remembering the weight of the world's suffering, to reach out with imagination and loving act into the ghettos and slums, the asylums and prisons, to neglected children and forgotten aged, and to all the unloved, unwanted victims of man's inhumanity; never to let our many blessings cause us to forget the many who are unblessed, the many who do without what we take so for granted. May our remembrance of this awaken our sluggish kindliness and send us forth to put our prayers into deeds.

"Thanks to the human heart by which we live,
Thanks to its tenderness, its joys, and fears,
To me the meanest flower that blows can give
Thoughts that do often lie too deep for tears."
—WILLIAM WORDSWORTH (1770-1850)

57 A MORE GENUINE MORALITY

"The sanctions of Sinai have lost their terrors, and people no longer accept the authority of Jesus even as a great moral teacher. Robbed of its supernatural supports, men find it difficult to take seriously a code of living that confessedly depended on them. 'Why shouldn't I?' or 'What's wrong with it?' are questions which in our generation press for an answer. And supranaturalist reasons — that God or Christ has pronounced it 'a sin' — have force, and even

meaning, for none but the diminishing religious remnant."
—JOHN ROBINSON (1919-   )

In his popular *Honest to God,* England's outspoken Anglican Bishop puts his finger on what so many nowadays interpret as widespread moral decline. We find little reason to believe that modern man is less ethical than his forefathers. But there is much moral confusion. In today's kaleidoscope of change, the moral codes of yesteryear prove inadequate. They were based, like the tribal taboos before them, on a stable rural culture. Now few live out their days in their native haunts, under the watchful eye of neighbors. The anonymity of urban life and the mobility industrialism has brought mean that the old prohibitions can be ignored with impunity. Proper behavior no longer can be imposed very effectively from without.

So comes the end of man's moral childhood. From now on, freed of old taboos, men will have to find new and better reasons for committing themselves to responsible ethical behavior. An ethical person is not one blindly obedient to a supernaturally sanctioned moral code. Rather, he is one who, having thoughtfully figured out what kind of behavior promotes human wellbeing, his own and society's, of his own volition faithfully makes this his own rule of conduct. He is one who has taught himself how to react consistently with compassion and fairness to others, how to postpone personal gratification of desires as long-range interests make necessary, how to act wisely, honestly, and considerately, not out of fear of punishment or hope of reward, but because he wants to live at peace with himself.

This transition will not be an easy one. Homo sapiens is but lately out of the jungle, and to domesticate and sublimate his brutal instincts is not a simple job, as history amply demonstrates. But we should have learned by now that reward and punishment don't turn the trick; externally imposed rules have failed rather badly in inculcating morality. Punish a child for stealing, what have you taught him? Perhaps only that stealing is wrong, *if* you get caught; at best, that stealing doesn't pay — a doubtful lesson, since in our society many forms of dishonesty generally pay off handsomely. Honesty is not often the best policy, not if one is referring to immediate material advantage. But then, real honesty is not prudence, nor expedience. Like courage, it is a rugged virtue, growing out of deep self-respect, and like all genuine morality an internal thing.

Given rapid urbanization, mushrooming population, our affluence, mobility, and consequent rootlessness, it would be surprising if our society showed no marked increase in deviant and lawless behavior. An historian notes that, after all, you'd hardly expect to find much juvenile delinquency in England in 1840, when most young children worked twelve hours a day. Where would they have found the energy? But our youngsters have it — the energy and the means. They live in a society most persuasively leading them into temptation at every turn. To jump to the conclusion that they are less moral than yesterday's industrial urchins seems a superficial judgment. They *do* have confused ideas of right and wrong — just like their elders.

When morality as obedience to divine rules collapses, the first stage is a kind of moral vacuum. Hopefully the next stage is the beginning of a more genuine kind of morality, one based not on rules but on love — that proper self-love which is self-respect, and that caring and consideration of others which values their wellbeing, autonomy, and growth.

Let's not mourn the passing of authoritarian morality, but get on with the constructive task. That is simply to grow up, and, more important, to help our children grow up, to be responsible for their lives, to internalize their moral principles, to win mastery over themselves, and hence over the power which knowledge now places in their hands.

"You can only make men free when they are inwardly bound by their own sense of responsibility."
—WILLIAM ERNEST HOCKING (1873-1966)

58 THE BEST THERAPY

"The foundation of medicine is love."
—PARACELSUS (1493?-1541)

We would be less surprised if this insight had come from a contemporary psychiatrist, rather than from this sixteenth century alchemist. We only begin to understand the healing powers of love. "Man does not live by bread alone," but by that spiritual bread which is love. Growth comes only from love, the love that is an active interest in others, and the genuine desire for their welfare. The unwanted, rejected child is hopelessly stunted; for parental love is to the infant what a mother bird's warmth is to her egg — the beneficent influence which gives the child power to peck through the shell of egocentricity.

The supreme lesson to be learned in life is the ability to love, to overbrim and overflow the walls of self. This is health, this is wholeness. "I love you," wrote Elizabeth Ferguson von Hesse, "not only for what you are but for what I am when I am with you. I love you not only for what you have made of yourself but what you are making of me. . . . I love you for ignoring the possibilities of the fool in me and laying firm hold of the possibilities of good in me." This is what being loved means. When another shows interest in us, confidence and faith in us, something deep within us responds. We respect ourselves more; we try to "measure up." It has been said that when someone loves us, it is as if he held a crown above our heads which henceforth we must try to grow tall enough to wear.

It is hard to exaggerate the transforming power of genuine love. Love may be counterfeit; we know the possessive, dominating attitude someone has called "smother love," and the egocentric, calculating "love" based upon dependency and submission. But real love is profoundly redemptive. If we doubt it, let us read again in Hugo's *Les Misérables* the story of the dramatic encounter of Monseigneur Bienvenu and Jean Valjean, the embittered victim of society, whose yellow passport was stamped "very dangerous." We cannot retell that story here, but we may recall the bishop's parting words: "Jean Valjean, my brother, you belong no longer to evil, but to good. It is your soul that I am buying for you. I withdraw it from dark thoughts and from the spirit of perdition, and I give it to God."

"Where there is hatred let me sow love; where there is injury, pardon; where there is doubt, faith; despair, hope; sadness, joy."
—FRANCIS OF ASSISI (1182-1226)

"You need not seek Him here or there. He is no farther off than the door of the heart."

—MEISTER ECKHART (1260-1327)

An ancient legend relates how God sought the safest place to hide the pearl of his divinity, away from man's restless curiosity. Rejecting in turn the highest mountain, the bowels of the earth, the dark recesses of the sea, he put it where man would be least likely to look — in man's own heart.

And man has sought afar for that which is the nearest of the near. His churches have steadily emphasized the sinfulness of man and the "otherness" of God. Often, not finding him "off there," men conclude he is not, and that man is but an alien and orphan in the universe. For one who fails to find divinity near at hand seldom finds it abroad.

Few things are more important in the religious life than the development of a certain inwardness. The liberal often says that conduct is basic to religion. But even more fundamental is the integrity and purity of motive from which good conduct springs.

So long as we lack inwardness, and have no more than a nodding acquaintance with ourselves, our morality is liable to be simply adherence to convention. We may speak the truth, but only because it is usually prudent to do so. We may observe current standards of right and wrong, but to gain approbation and social acceptance. Real truthfulness goes far beyond questions of policy, real virtue far transcends convention.

The prescription is not difficult to give. To follow it is. Be a pilgrim, not to some distant land, but in search of your own soul. "Enter thy closet and close the door." For, as Jesus said, "the kingdom of God is within you."

"Truth is within ourselves; it takes no rise
From outward things, whate'er you may believe.
There is an inmost centre in us all,
Where truth abides in fullness."

—ROBERT BROWNING (1812-89)

"Nor can that endure which has not its foundation upon love. For love alone diminishes not, but shines with its own light; makes an end of discord, softens the fires of hate, restores peace in the world, brings together the sundered, redresses wrong, aids all and injures none; and whoso invokes its aid will find peace and safety, and have no fear of future ill."

—ACT OF HORODLO (1413 A.D.)

The Greeks had a word for it, for the kind of love set forth in this ancient and remarkable statement, reputedly inspired by Queen Jadwiga of Poland. The Greeks called it "agapé:" we translate it "love," a word, alas, so loosely mouthed, so notoriously abused and overused that one wishes he might avoid it. Yet there really seems no way to do so, unless we simply adopt the Greek word itself.

Agapé was the seldom-used word that Paul employed in perhaps his greatest passage; not "eros" (from which we derive erotic) nor "philia" (philanthropy), but "agapé." Without agapé, he wrote to the squabbling, licentious converts in Corinth, a man is but a noisy gong, a clanging cymbal. Without agapé, knowledge, faith, charity, self-sacrifice are of nought avail. And then, as if realizing that the recipients of his letter wouldn't know what he was talking about, wouldn't understand in the least what agapé meant, he gave his classic definition: "Agapé is patient; agapé is kind and envies no one. It is never boastful, nor conceited, nor rude; never selfish, never irritated, never resentful. Agapé is gladdened by goodness, is slow to expose, is always eager to believe the best."

We might further expand the definition with other adjectives. Such love is disinterested, never transactional, never self-centered. It is willing and acting for the good of others, a response to their dignity, and to their reality. It is acting generously, but also realistically toward others.

Agapé, moreover, is the kind of love we have to learn. The infant starts life totally self-centered, and unable to cope with reality. Soon, finding his needs met, warmed, fed, comforted, he learns to coo in response, acquires the ability to respond to the sources of his well-being. He begins to love those who already love him. After a time he learns to love in the transactional sense; he discovers ways to please others, since by pleasing he can be surer of receiving what he wants and needs.

Meanwhile, the growing child gradually learns how to cope with reality, to distinguish between what he wishes were true and his private world of fantasy, and what happen to be the hard, stubborn facts of reality, including the reality of other people who, outside his family, he discovers, can be indifferent, manipulative, even cruel. He now must cope with people who have no intention of catering to his comfort and pleasure, who do not exist for his sake, and whom he must learn to meet where they are and treat as ends in themselves.

This learning comes hard; unlike hate, fear, and anger, and unlike love as sexual desire, agapé love does not come naturally, through our instincts. It is like a ladder we spend our lifetimes climbing, never managing to get to the top, yet hopefully mounting higher than its lowest rungs. Or we may liken love to a spectrum, a broad gamut running from "I'll scratch your back if you scratch mine," all the way up the line to such a statement as Jesus' from the cross: "Father, forgive them; they know not what they do." On this spectrum there is no clear point where "eros" and "philia" cease and "agapé" begins; for sexual love, romance, and friendship, though often only transactional, can also become fully expressive of agapé, the love that is other-oriented rather than self-seeking, that finds satisfaction in giving joy, without concern for immediate return, that genuinely desires the wellbeing and growth of the other.

It is a life-long task, this learning to be lovers; there are no easy routes, no "get there quick" techniques. But of this we can be confident: the inability to love is not a fixed, unchangeable aspect of our human nature. With patient perseverance we can overcome even the childhood deprivation that may have stunted our capacity to love. We can learn gradually to love, not in isolation but in community; not by pursuing unselfishness, but by pursuing reality, particularly the reality of other persons.

We too often stop, when reading *First Corinthians* 13, with the words, "and the greatest of these is love." We should continue with his next words: "Let your chief goal be love."

"It is good to give thanks to the Lord,
  to sing praises to thy name, O Most High;
To declare thy steadfast love in the morning,
  and thy faithfulness by night,
To the music of the lute and the harp,
  to the melody of the lyre.
For thou, O Lord, hast made me glad by thy work;
  at the work of thy hands I sing for joy."

—PSALM 92: 1-4

A favorite — and often quoted — saying of Margaret Fuller, the New England Transcendentalist, was: "I accept the universe." We are equally familiar with Carlyle's tart comment, when it was repeated to him: "Gad! She'd better!" Well, of course, we have to; we have no choice. But there is all the difference in the world *how* we "accept the universe," whether grudgingly or gladly, whether with dull submission or with enthusiasm. Miss Fuller meant the latter, that life is to be embraced. Her mood was the psalmist's.

There is a real difference of temperament here. Carlyle saw the seamy side of things; he felt the load of injustice, his ears were attuned to the dissonance of human misery. And just as all music is not gay gavottes and Mozartian allegros, so life has its dirges, clashing dissonances, and melancholy strains. There are grim inevitables which ethical sensitivity demands we accept only under protest. There are many wrongs to be righted, wounds to be healed, battles to be won.

Nevertheless, we side with Margaret Fuller. It is good to give thanks and sing for joy. This may not be the best of all possible worlds, but — thank God! — there is work to be done. Better than perfection is the striving for perfection; preferable to "heaven" is earth, with all its mingled light and dark, ugliness and beauty, joy and sorrow. Life is not a yoke to be borne; it is an adventure to be welcomed. It calls for high spirits, imagination, appreciation, enthusiasm. Whether with cheerful serenity or enthusiastic gladness, then, the wise man accepts the universe.

"Life is a struggle, but not a warfare; it is a day's labor, but labor on God's earth, under the sun and stars with other laborers, where we may think, and sing, and rejoice as we work."

—JOHN BURROUGHS (1837-1921)

62 THE ALL-PERVADING

"There is that by which all this world is pervaded."
—THE BHAGAVAD-GITA (500-200 B.C.)

We address the All-Pervading, not in a vain attempt to alter the operation of the universe; it is we who must change. It is we who need to listen to our own prayers, and how better to listen to what life has to teach us.

We see the All-Pervading in every moment, in the rich tapestry and overflowing cornucopia of nature; and in our answering gratitude, in our scorn for complaint and whimpering, in our knowledge that our lives are blessed beyond all deserving.

We recognize the All-Pervading, not through some ancient revelation, but in the monitions of our own consciences. We are drawn toward righteousness. There come moments when we are startled out of our complacency, when ideals we have forgotten return to us with compelling power; moments when as from some mountain-top, our view is extended, our normal horizons pushed way, way back.

We discover the All-Pervading in that which commands our loyalty, in our devotion to our families, our friends, and even to persons unknown to us; in our love of home and native land, and in the dawning recognition that we are all woven into a seamless garment of humanity, a steel-strong web of life.

In many ways we learn that, however inadequate and even childish are our thoughts, we can know and trust the All-Encompassing Power that continues the work of creation, that makes for righteousness, that resides in the world, and draws us ever toward higher loyalties and worthier endeavors.

63 HE CAME TO HIMSELF

"It is never too late to be wise."
—HENRI FRÉDÉRIC AMIEL (1821-81)

I always pause, when reading the parable of the Prodigal Son, over the words, "he came to himself." They reveal so clearly Jesus' estimate of human nature. Man is never sunk so low he may not

85

arise and return to his proper estate. The young man had sowed his wild oats; he had, as the recent translation renders it, "squandered his property in loose living." But his real self reasserts itself; through this bitter experience comes self-discovery. "I will arise and go to my father, and I will say to him, 'Father, I have sinned . . . I am no longer worthy to be called your son; treat me as one of your hired servants.' And he arose and came."

The discovery of one's higher potential, one's true self, is central to the religious endeavor. On whatever level we are now living, there is a higher level of which we are capable. The main obstacle is our complacency, a smug respectability. Emerson was right: we like to be settled — right also that only as we are unsettled is there any hope for us. And because we have a true, if only partially realized, self, we know we are not called to mediocrity, but to perpetual striving and growth. Beneath our contentment, a healthy self-dissatisfaction goads.

Let it goad; let the telling questions be asked: wherein do I betray myself, in what manner waste my substance? Am I building a more stately mansion "as the swift seasons roll," or slipping along in easy acquiescence with the world's standards? An honest self-inventory is not easy to take; if it be honest, it is painful. We have to make ourselves uncomfortable before we'll pull up stakes and resolutely strike out for higher country.

"Man is a choosing animal," said William James, "and his choice determines what he will become." We add John Dewey's words: "Growth itself is the moral end. Not perfection, but the enduring process of perfecting, maturing, refining, is the aim of living."

64   THE PARABLE OF TWO BROTHERS

"All men are brothers. All receive the blessings of the same heaven. The suffering of others is my suffering; the good of others is my good."

—A SHINTO TEXT

The Parable of the Prodigal Son is generally interpreted as an illustration of God's forgiveness of a repentant sinner. But if so, I wonder why Jesus introduced the Prodigal Son's brother? Jesus made his points with a minimum of words; he wasn't one to blurr the moral by unnecessarily complicating the story. Why, then, did he go on to tell about the older brother who was so resentful of his father's generous treatment of his sibling?

The answer might well be that Jesus' real point was not God's willingness to forgive repentant sinners. His primary audience, we are told, was a motley crowd of n'er-do-wells; but also gathered nearby were some Pharisees and doctors of the law, who "began grumbling among themselves: 'This fellow,' they said, 'welcomes sinners and eats with them.' " That their grumbling was quite audible is clear, for Jesus heard them. They were, shall we say, heckling him. Perhaps he was really addressing them in this story of the lad who squandered his inheritance, came to himself, and returned home a penniless penitent. His father welcomed him and called for a feast to celebrate the day: "For this son of mine was dead and has come back to life; he was lost and is found."

Only now does the older brother enter the scene. Coming in from the farm and hearing the festivities, he refuses to join the company. His father's pleading only unleashes an angry harangue: "You know how I have slaved for you all these years; I never once disobeyed your orders; and you never gave me so much as a kid, for a feast with my friends. But now that this son of yours turns up, after running through your money with his women, you kill the fatted calf for him."

We note the masterful use of the second person: "your son," not "my brother." The self-righteous hecklers, we imagine, did not fail to get the point. Santayana somewhere remarked that it is easier to make a saint out of a libertine than a prig. There is always hope for the darn fool who, hitting bottom, has the honesty to admit his mistakes, and the courage to try to repair the damage and build afresh. The many "older brothers" present a tougher problem, with their smugness, their hardened respectability. Self-righteousness is not attractive.

"The sages do not consider that making no mistakes is a blessing. They believe, rather, that the great virtue of man lies in his ability to correct his mistakes and continually to make a new man of himself."

—WANG YANG-MING (1472-1529)

65   THE ART OF BEING PRESENT

"There is only one world, the natural world, and only one truth about it; but this world has a spiritual life in it, which looks not to another world but to the beauty and perfection that this world suggests, approaches and misses."

—GEORGE SANTAYANA (1863-1952)

Being an absent-minded fellow, I would acquire the art of being present in the world, wholly there, attentive to the vitality and quality of each living moment as it flows out of the future and into the past.

O thou who art the heartbeat of life, I would recognize and cherish the wonder of each new day. Let me learn to be fully alive and alert, to be wholly and solely myself, and wide awake between sleep and sleep. When I absently turn away from love, from beauty, from human need, and grow preoccupied with trivial concerns and superficial wants, let something always reawaken me to recognition of the depth and wonder of this reality that surrounds me, that beckons to me. When I am agitated or anxious, annoyed or distracted, let me remember the way back to inner quiet and serenity.

66   PROPER PRIDE

"I believe in pride . . . a pride that prays ever for an awareness of that borderline where, unless watchful of yourself, you cross over into arrogance, into vanity, into mirror gazing, into misuse and violation of the sacred portions of your personality."

—CARL SANDBURG (1878-1967)

Pride is the first and deadliest of the seven deadly sins. At least, such excessive, overweening pride as the Greeks called "hubris." This is the kind of pride that enabled Mussolini to write in his *Autobiography*: "In every hour of my life it is the spiritual element that leads me on . . . I have annihilated in myself every egoism." Any man who can so describe himself is on dangerous ground. In fact, as we noted in an earlier reading, we may well suspect that such conceit is a cover-up for feelings of inferiority and self-hate.

People who seem to possess an exaggerated sense of superiority may be only masquerading their wretched feelings of inadequacy. Some estimate that at least ninety per cent of the population actually suffer gnawing feelings of inferiority; feel they lack social poise, are unloved; fear failure. Hence, they are afraid to be themselves, to be open.

The problem of human pride is not as simple as the Greek playwrights, Hebrew prophets, and Christian theologians have traditionally made it. Arrogance is indeed unlovely, and the source of untold misery. Man's propensity for self-delusion is great and widespread. Each of us is prone to paint a self-portrait that eliminates the blemishes and shows our better features to advantage. The conquest of ego-centricity is the great battle of our personal lives. But is the cause of ego-centricity self-love, or feelings of personal inadequacy?

Traditionally men have thought that the trouble is that men think too well of themselves. Hence they have preached self-negation, self-abasement. It is a modern insight, and a sound one, that most of us do not think well enough of ourselves, that we lack a healthy, realistic self-image, a wholesome self-esteem. Lack of self-confidence and self-respect is perhaps the greatest handicap in life for most people.

The goal is to think well of oneself, but not too well; to recognize one's strength without forgetting one's weaknesses; to accept one's limitations with good grace; to be able to acknowledge past mistakes and present short-comings without lingering and exaggerated feelings of guilt and remorse; to know when we have punished ourselves enough that it is time to forgive and forget.

67 THE AUTOBIOGRAPHY OF MANKIND

"Out of the poetic need, which is one of the spirit, all religions have been born, and by the poetic grace the divine spark is kept eternally alight within the human flint."

—ST.-JOHN PERSE (1889-   )

Art and religion are old allies. Who can say whether art gave birth to religion, or religion to art? Worship has been called the mother of the arts, and the all-comprehending art. And art has aptly been called the autobiography of mankind.

What our grandparents were able to draw from their daily reading of a chapter or two from the Bible, or from one of the classics of devotional literature, we too can find in the great treasure-house of art. I do not suggest that the Bible, or Saint Augustine, or Quaker John Woolman cannot continue to sustain and quicken the inner vision for a great many people. But for those to whom they no longer seem to serve in keeping alight the divine spark "within the human flint," there are other resources, an embarrassment of riches. I do not refer simply, or primarily, to art labelled "religious," for all significant art represents a distillation of life, a record of human experience. The most gifted and perceptive members of our race have found, through their art, ways of saying "yes" to the agony and ecstacy, the mystery and marvel of being human. Schweitzer called Bach "the greatest of preachers." He was at least a tremendous one, able to communicate the sacred through the universal language of music. So all true artists respond to the pain and beauty and incredibility of existence, each in his own way, by creating a poem, a painting, or a sonata. We, less gifted, can see more deeply into life as we learn to look through their eyes.

The arts are no mere appenda to life, an ornamentation growing out of leisure and surplus. They are for civilizing man. By creating works of art, men seek to clarify and extend their vision, and to communicate it. The artist sees into life a little further than the rest of us. He can teach us to perceive more. He can awaken our realization that nothing in life is ordinary or commonplace, that every moment is unique and revelatory to the spirit attuned to the perpetual miracle of being.

True, the arts do provide us with gracious entertainment and a way of partially escaping the harsh realities. They can give us vicarious experiences of adventure and romance. More seriously, they can raise powerful witness against social evils and injustices; witness Dickens' novels, Markham's "Man with a Hoe," or Kathe Kollwitz' drawings. Paintbrush as well as pen can be mightier than the sword. But the basic, indispensable purpose of the arts is for the deepening of life. As Robert Frost put it: "Poetry begins in delight, and ends in wisdom." The arts provide one of the main ways we have of becoming more fully human, more fully alive and imaginative. The painter, sculptor, composer, no less than the writer, extend and intensify our vision of life, our ability to see, hear, and feel what we might never experience in many lifetimes, left entirely to our own resources.

Here, then, is all the artistic heritage, available to guide and stimulate us in our pursuit of wisdom and abundant life. Never before has art been so available to everyone. The masterpieces of music are on record and tape; those of painting in surprisingly satisfactory reproductions. City dwellers have all the resources of large public libraries at their disposal, as well as magnificent museums. The small town library is able to borrow from its big city sisters. Quite without money we can explore this wealth until we find what arts and artists are most effective door-openers for us, best able to quicken our imaginations and awaken powerful response. Any man is rich who "owns" the autobiography of mankind.

68   AN INIMITABLE MIXTURE
OF INGENUITY AND STUPIDITY

"Man has mounted science, and is now run away with. I firmly believe that before many centuries more, science will be the master of man. The engines he will have invented will be beyond his strength to control. Someday science may have the existence of man in its power, and the human race may commit suicide by blowing up the world."

—HENRY JAMES (1843-1916)

What prescience! It takes less foresight now to see that mankind is on "collision course," and that our race will probably be done in by its own inimitable mixture of ingenuity and stupidity. Yet we cannot abandon hope, cannot give up on the proposition that what man has gotten himself into, he can get himself out of, if he will.

Homo sapiens has lessons to learn. This bloodiest of centuries should drive home that war is no longer tolerable, that absolute national sovereignty has become dangerously anachronistic, and that mankind's only appropriate war from now on is against war itself, and against all that jeopardizes earth's future.

It may be that science has indeed got us in its power. If so, the human race, if it does not "commit suicide by blowing up the world," will suffer the slower but no less inexorable fate of planetary exhaustion. We are not ready to grant that this is inevitable. What we do believe is that we twentieth-century Americans are on an economic binge, a fantastic joyride, squandering irreplaceable natural resources. Tragically, most of us like it. We like the prosperity, the fat pay envelopes, the Christmas stocking full of goodies and gadgets, the shiny overpowered cars and color television sets, and a hundred other toys for grown-ups we can buy with all this green manna, courtesy of the military-industrial complex.

The Good Earth has been a tolerant mother. But it is time we learned how precious, and how vulnerable, is this planet's envelope of air, its thin layer of fertile soil, its silent factories of green forests and lush prairies and sunlit oceans, where the miraculous regeneration of the atmosphere goes on via the plant kingdom's photosynthetic productivity. Plato long ago wrote that deforestation and overgrazing had brought down civilizations before his own. We speak nowadays of "under-developed countries;" most of them, more accurately, are "over-developed," a polite word for "ruined by unsound agricultural practices." Many barren lands were once virtual Edens.

But until man "mounted science, and is now run away with," the total ecological balance of nature was never seriously threatened. Now our knowledge explosion has given the means of committing planetary suicide. Scientists are not evil men — no more so than the rest of us; and knowledge in itself is not evil. But the indiscriminate application of it is. It is evil to make atomic weapons, evil to produce poisonous gases, evil to waste earth's fertility and mineral wealth, evil to pollute its streams and lakes and oceans. It is evil to make anything without taking careful thought for the consequences, especially when the consequences may be contributing to the death of the planet itself.

Winston Churchill called himself an optimist, saying he had never figured it made much sense to be anything else. We too hold to a tenacious optimism. We believe it is not too late, that mankind still has a future, a chance. But such a belief only makes sense if we are willing to translate it into action. Let everyone ask himself: What am I doing to restore the balance of nature, to cure man's warring madness, and to make science the servant rather than the master of man?

"It is not enough to find new institutions; we must change ourselves, our characters, our moral-political wills . . . Whoever goes on living as before has not grasped the menace . . . The change can come only in every man's manner of living. Every little act, every word, every attitude in millions and billions of people matter."

—KARL JASPERS (1883-1969)

69   LIKE THE RUSH OF MIGHTY WATERS

"Let the spirit banish all that disturbs; let the body that envelops it be still, and all the frettings of the body, and all that surrounds it; let the earth and sea and air be still, and heaven itself. And then let the man think of the spirit as streaming, pouring, rushing and shining into him from all sides while he stands quiet."

—PLOTINUS (204?-270)

Such mental images have proved very helpful. The philosophic effort is to form right ideas about Ultimate Reality. But the worshipper seeks positive experience of the all-environing unity in which we have our being. Now, retired from daily occupation and companionship, can you become sensible of that which is beyond the power of the senses, and see that which is invisible, feel that which is intangible? "There is nothing more evident than that which cannot be seen by the eyes and nothing more palpable than that which cannot be perceived by the senses," we read in *The Golden Mean of Tsesze* — words attributed to Confucius. And again: "The power of spiritual forces in the universe — how active it is everywhere! Invisible to the eyes, and impalpable to the senses, it is inherent in all things, and nothing can escape its operation . . . Like the rush of mighty waters, the presence of the unseen Powers is felt; sometimes above us, sometimes around us . . . Such is the evidence of things invisible that it is impossible to doubt the spiritual nature of man."

Then let each of us ask: Am I aware that such is my nature, aware who I am? Is my spirit tuned to the impalpable? Do I really believe in the present activity of unseen powers? Do I confidently expect to find God?

"The way to worship," Rufus Jones advised, "is to cultivate the habit of worship; the way to find God is to expect to find Him; the way to be flooded with the Divine Presence is to set the will and disposition open in that direction."

70   EFFECTUAL PRAYER

"Prayer fails because to the soul there was no real presence of God while we were praying."

—JOHN HAMILTON THOM (1808-94)

Not to believe in prayer, it has been suggested, is failure to believe in the hopes and dreams and aspirations of men. Prayer is the hoping, dreaming, aspiring of men, the upward reaching of their spirits. It is, in Emerson's words, "contemplation of the facts of life from the highest point of view . . . the soliloquy of a beholding and jubilant soul . . . But prayer as a means to effect a private end is meanness and theft." There is, then, prayer, and prayer. And we have often allowed ourselves to judge it on its lowest, meanest level — petitions for external things. On its highest levels it is asking for nothing, it is praise and adoration and silent communion, and the patient, honest endeavor to discern our truest and highest course of action.

Among much wise counsel on prayer from the pen of a nineteenth-century English Unitarian leader, J.H. Thom, the following is particularly worthy of thoughtful consideration: "The first condition of effectual prayer is that we do not speak into empty space, that the awe of the great Presence is upon us, that the mighty Shadow has circled us in, the Spirit brooding on our souls in a sense of One very nigh in whom love and holiness are perfect — and that then we speak, if we speak at all, only as we are moved, only that which we should dare to speak if we stood before his face and saw the majesty of God . . . It is an act of the highest irreverence to dare to speak to God without first carefully drawing nigh unto him, and seeking by collectedness of being to be penetrated through and through by the sense of what he is."

Remembering the irreverence of many public prayers, and the thoughtless, inattentive repetition of rote prayers we ourselves have often been guilty of, we find Dr. Thom's first condition most pertinent. If it were more generally observed, skepticism regarding prayer would greatly diminish. Then let us resolve to observe it ourselves.

94

"Always decide to use humble love. If you resolve on that once for all, you may subdue the whole world."
> —FEODOR MIKHAILOVICH DOSTOEVSKI (1821-81)

So speaks Father Zossima, in *The Brothers Karamazov.* We note particularly the verbs: "decide," "resolve." Love is not simply an emotion; it is also a fundamental principle to be applied. Young couples, discussing the marriage vows, often express their reluctance to promise to love. They thus reveal their misunderstanding of what it is they are being asked to promise each other. What they cannot properly promise is that they will always be *in love.* Even in the best of marriages, the partners cannot always expect to be madly in love. But the marriage vow is asking them to resolve once for all to work together in building a relationship that will hopefully continue to grow in depth, in richness, in stability, through the years.

As in marriage, so in parents' relationship to their children, we are to "make love our aim," our settled intent; loving them not sentimentally, or selflessly, but realistically — that is, always as real persons in their own right, never as some sort of projection of ourselves.

Jesus carried this to its extreme, calling upon his followers to love even their enemies — especially their enemies, since who needs love so badly as the man who hates you and persecutes you. Most of us are still too far from sainthood to think we can ever achieve such love as this. But we do know that others have, that small minority deservedly called "saints."

Our goal can be more modest: Just to make it to the next higher rung, by following as best we can Father Zossima's excellent counsel: always being careful to foster in ourselves "an actively benevolent love."

"Brothers," said the old priest, "love is a teacher; but one must know how to acquire it, for it is hard to acquire, it is dearly bought, it is won slowly by long labor. Everyone can love occasionally, even the wicked. But we must love not only occasionally, for a moment, but for ever."

We can grow in our capacity for loving, by resolving that we shall, by making it our fixed aim. And whenever we succeed in reaching out with patience and kindness, without malice or envy, to the reality of another person, friend or stranger, or even enemy, we become more fully human ourselves, and more productive of that agapé love so desperately needed, if man "the killer ape" is ever to become the successful builder of an earthly paradise.

So let us resolve, once for all, to make love our aim, our chief goal, our first order of business. If we succeed in this, we have succeeded in life, however badly we fare by material standards. And if we fail in this, there is no other success that can compensate.

72   THINK ON THESE THINGS

"The soul is dyed in the color of its thoughts."
—MARCUS AURELIUS (121-180)

A former political prisoner of the Nazis, inmate of Dachau, has testified that what helped him most to maintain his sanity and to keep alive a flickering candle of hope was the fact that from early childhood he had made a practice of memorizing favorite passages; and now, deprived of books, he was a living library. At any moment, he could recall lines of Goethe or Schiller, a passage from Shakespeare, the wisdom of Marcus Aurelius or Epictetus, the timeless words of Isaiah or Jesus. From the filth and brutality and hopelessness of the concentration camp, he could journey at will to the homes of the great and good. Starved in body, he could nourish his spirit on wholesome thoughts, on some of the world's best thinking memorably expressed. Returning from such mental pilgrimage, he had sufficient perspective to save him from cynicism and despair. Thus he helped not only himself, but some of his fellow victims.

Heaven forbid that we should ever have such dire need of a well-stocked mind. But the free spirit, facing today's totalitarianisms and the extreme reaction of "right" and "left," must reckon realistically with the possibility of such a fate. And short of the concentration camp, other misfortunes can bar us from the world's libraries — failing eyesight, for example.

An equal case for memorizing significant bits of literature can be made without reference to extreme possibilities. The wise Roman emperor outlined the argument, as did Buddha in the *Dhammapada,* when he taught: "All that we are is the result of what we have thought . . . It is good to tame the mind, which is difficult to hold in and flighty, rushing wherever it listeth." The Bible adds its testimony: "As a man thinketh in his heart, so is he." Well, then, let us think the best thoughts. How better than by nourishing our minds on the world's wisdom, on great Bible passages, favorite poems, and wise sayings. Well-chosen words, thoroughly memorized, are truly acquired; they become our property, yes, and in due season, they become us.

"A man can stand a lot as long as he can stand himself. He can live without hope, without books, without friends, without music, as long as he can listen to his own thoughts."
—AXEL MARTIN FREDRIK MUNTHE (1857-1949)

73   MEMORY

"You say the first words of the old song and I finish the line and the stanza. But where do I have them, or what becomes of them when I am not thinking of them for months and years, that they should lie so still, as if they did not exist, and yet so nigh that they come on the instant when they are called for?"
—RALPH WALDO EMERSON (1803-82)

In a universe where everything seems incredible, human memory is surely one of the most remarkable of our attributes. Most of our mental activity depends upon it. He who loses his memory, loses himself. Without the ability to recall the past, our own and that of our race, life becomes incoherent, a meaningless sequence. Yet we have but the scantiest inkling of how human memory functions. We only know that on seeing a face, we are aware that we have seen it before; on hearing a fact, we recognize that we already know it.

To be sure, we also experience the opposite of what Emerson described. The words of the old song don't come. Or the name of an old friend eludes us. We do forget, or seem to. Perhaps, however, we never really forget anything we have thoroughly learned and genuinely appropriated into ourselves. Studies have indicated that no significant experience is ever completely lost. Under patient inquiry, long forgotten events, facts, names, can often be revived. Psychoanalysis, for example, demonstrates how much of what is apparently quite forgotten is only, like a buried city, awaiting the "archeologist" who, with infinite pains, will dig it out. Experiments with hypnosis likewise reveal how much of what we appear to have forgotten are in fact memories that have only slipped beyond immediate recall. But we need not undergo Analysis or experiment with hypnosis to realize that memories are not easily destroyed; all we need do is to pay attention to our dreams. How often we dream of a childhood friend whom we haven't seen or even thought of in many years, yet in our dream he is vivid, clearly identifiable, as surely himself as ever? How often we recall, perhaps because of some slender hint, some passing comment, an incident long dormant, apparently forgotten?

Memory is often, all too often, an exasperating servant. We can't recall the title of a book read only last week. The name we know perfectly well won't come. We reach for a fact only to discover we've mis-filed it. We curse our bad memories. If only we could come up with that apt quotation, that telling argument, that charming story, how wise and witty we should appear. The frequent failures of this extraordinary faculty, one suspects, often obscure what a miracle it is that the past should live on in us, and work for us.

Or against us. We don't mean to overlook the negative side. Everyone suffers in some measure from childhood traumas. There are many things we'd like to forget, if only we could. To be assured that we haven't really forgotten, but have only repressed the memory of unpleasant, even devastating, personal experiences, is not comforting news. Everyman is somewhat victimized by his past.

But here we would accentuate the positive. In large measure, our memory does work for us, and bless us. We should be totally lost without it. So let us treasure the extraordinary ability which allows us to recall at will so much that has enriched our lives.

"The thought of our past years . . . doth breed Perpetual benediction."
—WILLIAM WORDSWORTH (1770-1850)

"First of all have patience . . . You will disturb your development in a most violent manner if you expect answers from outside to questions which only the most secret feelings of your calmest hours can solve. I beg you to be patient to all the unsolved problems of your heart and to care for the questions themselves. Do not search for answers to be given you; if given, they would be of no use, for you could not live them. For the present live in the questions and little by little and almost unconsciously you will enter the answers and live them also."

—RAINER MARIA RILKE (1875-1926)

Patience is an undramatic virtue, but much needed and most difficult. We usually think of it in terms of daily vexations and irritations. The German poet here relates it to the fundamental questions, like the ones raised by Job. What is the meaning of life? How can one reconcile the goodness of God with the evil and tragedy of life? There are no easy answers to such questions. Facile answers are given, of course. Many, perhaps most, think they have keys to the unsolved riddles, merely because they have embraced some creed or memorized some catechism. But in the deeper sense the poet is right: answers given are of no use, for we cannot live them.

We must come to our own answers. How? By living with the questions. To find meaning of one's life, to discover one's true vocation, to meet one's God and know him "otherwise than by hearsay," to make peace with the existence of evil — these are indeed enterprises requiring time, and patience. They are questions no one else can properly answer for us; they must be asked again and again; we must not evade them or shunt them aside. Life is a deeply mysterious business; beware the man who claims to know too much. The wisest man is the humblest. Instead of seeking answers from outside yourself, cultivate your patience, learn to live in your questions, trusting that gradually perhaps even imperceptibly, your answers will emerge, real answers that you can live.

"In walking, just walk; in sitting, just sit; above all, don't wobble."

—YUN-MEN WEN-YEN (?-949 A.D.)

> *"I have learned*
> *To look on nature not as in the hour*
> *Of thoughtless youth but hearing oftentimes*
> *The still, sad music of humanity,*
> *Nor harsh nor grating, though of ample power*
> *To chasten and subdue."*
>
> —WILLIAM WORDSWORTH (1770-1850)

How much we feel the tragic sense of life no doubt depends upon our temperament and our experience. But even if we are of fairly even disposition and inclined to optimism, and even if fortune has smiled upon us, we cannot wholly escape feeling the weight of human misery. Nor have we any right to be deaf to "the still, sad music of humanity." Hunger, disease, poverty stalk our world. Cruel discriminations blight the lives of many. Man's "inhumanity to man" takes its fearful toll. Those who work in state hospitals, or visit as volunteers, can testify to the multitude and wretchedness of the forgotten aged. Or, if we grow dull to the tragic sense of life, a trip to any public institution for the mentally retarded will bring us up hard against reality.

It is not the role of religion to bring comfort and "peace of mind" to the individual, to the neglect of social responsibility and ethical sensitivity to the sorrow and sufferings of others. Our faith should fortify us against disaster and the fear of misfortune. But it should also challenge us to minister to the needs of others. In our world, made one neighborhood by human ingenuity, there can be no boundaries to our sympathies nor any place for indifference.

Hearing the "still, sad music of humanity," and moved to acts of compassion, we are fortunate if we can go on with the poet. For there is also a happy sense of life; there is health as well as disease, laughter as well as tears, ecstasy as well as heartbreak. And there is also the deeper intuition of the heart, subdued and chastened, that sings, like the nightingale's song heard all night.

> *"And I have felt*
> *A presence that disturbs me with the joy*
> *Of elevated thoughts; a sense sublime*
> *Of something far more deeply interfused,*

Whose dwelling is the light of setting suns,
And the round ocean and the living air,
And the blue sky, and in the mind of man."

—WORDSWORTH

76   THE DUTY OF HAPPINESS

"There is no duty we so much underrate as the duty to be happy."
—ROBERT LOUIS STEVENSON (1850-94)

We are beholden to Stevenson, not only for *Treasure Island, Kidnapped* and *A Child's Garden of Verses,* and much else, but also for this one sentence. It contains basic wisdom. We Americans are used to thinking of happiness as a right to be pursued. A useful corrective is to see happiness as a duty; and unhappiness as a sin — or, if you prefer, the result of wrong thinking, wrong values, faulty relationships: to life, to one's fellowmen, and to oneself. Unhappiness is as surely a sign that one is on the wrong road, as fever is a symptom that one is ill.

The unhappy person needs to ask himself, as honestly as he can: "What is wrong with me? Not with the world, not with those other people, but with me." He needs to stop trying to fill the vacuum in his life by seeking diversion, by pursuing pleasure, by trying to have fun. For unhappiness is not caused by things external, or lack of what is truly needful. Sorrow, yes, this we may know; and discomfort and pain and disappointment. But the cause of unhappiness lies in oneself; or, if that is too sweeping a statement, the best place to start looking for the cause is not out there, but inside ourselves.

Alexander Magoun, in his "The Nature of Happiness," quotes a German businessman who had been tortured in Dachau and Buchenwald by the Nazis, before finally escaping. This was the wisdom he had garnered from that experience: "There are always compensations. The only real prison any man knows is himself. The Gestapo tried to make life additionally hard to bear for the more intelligent by having them collect the garbage and empty the slop jars. All the professors were assigned to this job, and I was made to join them because I had a Ph.D. Actually, it became the one happy experience in my imprisonment because of the conversations we had about history, philosophy, politics, and our observations of how the place was affecting the guards, ourselves, and our fellow prisoners. You make your own happiness."

Two sentences in this quotation seem especially significant: "The only real prison any man knows is himself," and "You make your own happiness." This is the truth: We are responsible for our own happiness or unhappiness. And if this be not entirely true, it is largely so. Many things, and many people, can give us pleasure, amusement, occasionally even joy. But we must create our own happiness, by choosing a way of life, the kind of values, the commitments and relationships that make a positive contribution to our love of life, our sense of personal worth, our peace of mind, and our acceptance of the riddles and disappointments and tragedies that are an inevitable part of living.

The man who chooses a way of life that leads toward happiness does not expect the impossible from life, the answer to its mysteries, evils, and injustices. But these things — even these — do not destroy his love of life, and his trust that behind or within life's tragedies and enigmas there shines a light, there flows a living water. Such a man knows that happiness must be earned, by deserving it; that it depends on the development of inner resources, on one's appreciation of beauty, one's sensitivity to the needs of others, one's determination to meet life's vicissitudes with courage and to live each day to the full.

Albert Camus had a brave, defiant answer to the unhappiness so prevalent in our mixed-up, war-torn world: In protest, we must create happiness. Robert Louis Stevenson, a man of greater peace of mind, though no stranger to life's darker side, said much the same thing, but less defiantly. Hold on to his thought, and ponder it: "There is no duty we so much underrate as the duty to be happy."

"Do not pray for easy lives. Pray to be stronger men. Do not pray for tasks equal to your powers. Pray for powers equal to your tasks. Then every day you will wonder at yourself, at the richness of life that has come to you."

—PHILLIPS BROOKS (1835-93)

"When you don't feel the way you ought to act, if you just act the way you ought to feel, then you WILL *feel the way you ought to act."*

—WILLIAM JAMES (1842-1910)

"Deep within us all there is an amazing inner sanctuary of the soul, a holy place, a Divine Center, a speaking Voice, to which we may continuously return. Eternity is at our hearts, pressing upon our time-torn lives, warming us with intimations of an astounding destiny, calling us home unto Itself. Yielding to these persuasions, gladly committing ourselves in body and soul, utterly and completely, to the Light Within, is the beginning of true life. It is a dynamic center, a creative Life that presses to birth within us."
—THOMAS R. KELLY (1893-1941)

Pondering these lines from *A Testament of Devotion,* an already widely beloved modern Quaker classic, I keep returning to the phrase "a dynamic center." Why, I wonder, has the symbol of the wheel been so markedly ignored, since it makes such a striking analogy to our lives? Indeed, the problem of personal religion is always to find a hub into which all the various spokes of our lives may fit. If the rim of the wheel is made to stand for the circumference of our lives as we come into contact with the world, and the spokes for the varied and multiple activities that occupy our days, then it follows that our lives are only true and strong and balanced when each spoke is fastened securely to the hub.

The spokes go off in all directions; and so do our activities and interests. At worst, our lives are in the plight of the schoolboy's Caesar who "jumped on his horse and rode off in all directions at once." But each spoke, whatever way it points, performs a necessary function in the total wheel — so long as it properly stems from the center. Life, without varied and even conflicting interests, cannot be well balanced and well rounded. And tied into a hub, these apparently unrelated, seemingly contradictory elements form an orderly, meaningful pattern. Our lives become a wheel, capable of moving toward a goal.

How can such a radical centering of our lives be achieved? That center, that focus, lies "deep within us all." It cannot be found in anything external, neither a god far off, nor an authoritative church, nor an infallible book. It has to be found as men withdraw periodically, train themselves to stillness, and cultivate an inner listening ear.

"From within or from behind," wrote Emerson, "a light shines

through us upon things and makes us aware that we are nothing,
but the light is all."

*"For this is the journey that men make: to find themselves. If
they fail in this, it doesn't matter much what else they find. Money,
position, fame, many loves, revenge are all of little consequence,
and when the tickets are collected at the end of the ride they are
tossed into a bin marked failure. But if a man happens to find
himself — if he knows what he can be depended upon to do, the
limits of his courage, the position from which he will no longer
retreat, the degree to which he can surrender his inner life to some
woman, the secret reservoirs of his determination, the extent of his
dedication, the depth of his feeling for beauty, his honest and
unpostured goals — then he has found a mansion which he can
inhabit with dignity all the days of his life."*

—JAMES A. MICHENER (1907-   )

78   THE ART OF LISTENING

*"The British don't really like music; they don't know anything
about it. They just adore the noise it makes."*

—THOMAS BEECHAM (1879-1961)

Recently I visited a brand new house whose owner proudly
explained that every room from basement to attic was fully wired
for sound. As he spoke, music filled the air; it seemed to come from
all sides. Acoustically it was a fine job, well-balanced, with higher
fidelity than one one generally hears in a concert hall; all in all, a
small engineering triumph. At least, he told me so; and I did not
doubt it, though as he kept talking, and all the other guests were
busily chatting, I couldn't really listen to the music, or more than
half hear it. I found myself thinking of Sir Thomas Beecham's tart
exclamation, and wondering how often this family actually
listened to the music they made their constant audient
environment. Did they truly love music, or did they "just adore the
noise it makes?"

Modern technology makes magnificent recorded music readily
available. It has also revealed that a great many people don't really
like it; they seldom actually listen to it. They chiefly use it as a way
of blotting out silence, a way of not paying attention. To love

music must mean, first of all, to have cultivated the art of listening to it; it must mean willingness to pay it the compliment of giving full attention to it. It is not enough to treat it with the disrespect we show when we use it as background for conversation, or as a means of escaping from ourselves. I do not suggest that we should always be engaged in intellectual analysis of it, though this can help us learn the art of listening. But it does mean that when we listen, we try to give it our full attention.

As with music, so with people. If we are with a person, we ought to be fully with him; we ought to enter comprehendingly into his world and make encounter. There is close linkage between listening and loving, as Erich Fromm and others have pointed out. Successful psychotherapy depends heavily on the therapist's ability to listen; to hear what the person seeking help says, and what he cannot say outright, but can only reveal unknowingly — what he does not quite have the courage to say, what he does not know how to say, what he doesn't even recognize that he thinks or feels. Psychiatric listening is both an arduous and a delicate art. The therapist, hearing the other at various levels, encourages the recognition of important insights. He literally enables the other person to listen to himself and to hear what the deeper, forgotten parts of his nature are trying to tell him.

You and I are not called upon to become amateur psychotherapists. Let us not "rush in like fools where angels fear to tread." But we can practice the art of listening. We can recognize the close relationship between listening and loving, and train ourselves to be more attentive. To listen to a person is to grant him respect. It is worth remembering that the word "respect" does not mean fear or awe, but rather denotes the ability to see a person as he is. Respect derives from the Latin "respicere," meaning "to look at." To respect a person is to look at him, to pay attention to him, really to listen to him.

We cannot love all mankind, except in the most abstract way. Jesus did not teach, "Thou shalt love all men." He said, "Thou shalt love thy neighbor." We can love humanity only as we meet it in the never-ending stream of individuals who cross our path. We love mankind when we are not indifferent to the concerns of those near us, both friend and stranger; as we pay attention, cultivate awareness, and make ourselves sensitively available.

"If you keep still and listen, things will always explain themselves. It is as if something drew near you and revealed itself — something that holds itself at a distance when you don't listen."

—STEWART EDWARD WHITE (1873-1946)

79   THE PRACTICE OF THE PRESENCE

"He was never hasty nor loitering, but did each thing in its season, with an even, uninterrupted composure and tranquility of spirit. 'The time of business,' he said, 'does not with me differ from the time of prayer, and in the noise and clatter of my kitchen, while several persons are at the same time calling for different things, I possess God in as great tranquility as if I were upon my knees at the Blessed Sacrament.' "

—BROTHER LAWRENCE (1611-91)

These closing words of the Fourth Conversation in *The Practice of the Presence of God* betray why this seventeenth-century devotional tract continues to appeal. All of us would like to learn the secret of maintaining tranquility in the midst of the distractions and pressures of our lives.

It is a timely reminder, that the time of business should not "differ from the time of prayer." Religion is not one activity amongst many. Religion is "all deeds and all reflection," a way of living in continuing recollection of one's supreme ideals, the distinction between sacred and secular obliterated since even the humblest duty — the washing of pans, the mending of socks, the hoeing of one's garden — becomes a sacramental act. This is Paul's prayer without ceasing: not the prayer of words, nor any outward act, but the recollection that, by virtue of our divine kinship, we are forever as close to God as we will to be.

If God is, he is everywhere present. He is not an occasional visitor, nor ever more truly present than at this very instant. He is always ready to flow into our hearts; indeed, he is there now — it is we who are absent. If we would make him real in our lives, and find tranquility of heart, steadiness of purpose, and each hour suffused with joy and meaning, we should, like Brother Lawrence, train ourselves to turn hour by hour to him "in whom we live and move and have our being," train ourselves to live from the deeper levels of our hearts, from our divine center.

"He who does not practice devotion has neither intelligence nor reflection. And he who does not practice reflection has no calm. How can a man without calm obtain happiness? When a man's heart follows his roaming senses, it snatches away his spiritual knowledge as a wind does a ship on the waves."

—THE BHAGAVAD-GITA, Chapter 2, 66-67 (300-200 B.C.)

80   OUR HEARTH, OUR HOME

"Go where he will, the wise man is at home,
His hearth the earth, his hall the azure dome;
Where his clear spirit leads him, there's his road,
By God's own light illumined and foreshadowed."

—RALPH WALDO EMERSON (1803-82)

There was always a chapter from the Bible before we left the breakfast table at my Quaker grandmother's. Although I never objected, it was a habit I did not acquire. But it did serve a purpose; like the silent grace before the meal, it was a reminder, even if we did not always heed it.

Few read the Bible any more. And unfortunately few have ever found an adequate substitute; for example, the acquaintance of the great poets. "Poetry," as Wallace Stevens rightly insisted, "is a response to the daily necessity of getting the world aright." That man is probably fooling himself who recognizes no such necessity. There is no standing still in life. Whoever is not growing is dying. Whoever neglects to cultivate his ethical sensitivity and aesthetic appreciation is but letting the soul's garden become choked with weeds.

We advocate therefore making friends with whatever literature we discover serves us best in the life-long task of growing up toward ethical and spiritual maturity — such writing as can help us feel at home in this world, the earth our hearth, the azure dome our hall. Take, for example, the Japanese poets, those masters of the art of Haiku, who set "the world aright" by the simplest of means — just seventeen syllables. Much modern poetry is hard to understand; some poets we suspect even aim at incomprehensibility. Not so, at least, the masters of Haiku.

"What happiness to wake, alive again,
Into this same grey world of winter rain."

So wrote Shôha. Only fourteen common words, but good tonic for a raw, wet morning. Or, what wisdom in Basho's lines:

"Though veiled amid these misty showers of grey,
Fuji is lovelier still — unseen today."

Anyone is the richer for tucking a hundred Haiku firmly into his memory, for use as needed to "chase the blues," to rout self-pity, or to restore his visual sensitivity.

More than this, we advocate trying our hand at creating these poetic vignettes. Really good ones are not easily come by, but the effort teaches appreciation, and, persisted in, may help us toward the serentiy and wisdom these venerable eastern poets had learned so well.

81 HE THAT HATH EYES, LET HIM SEE

"When I look at the sun, you say to me, "What do you see? Do you not see a yellow disk the size of a guinea?" "No! no! no!" I answer, "I see an innumerable company of the heavenly host, crying Holy, Holy, Holy is the Lord God Almighty!" . . . I look through my eyes, not with them."

—WILLIAM BLAKE (1757-1827)

Where the materialist sees only a golden guinea, a mystical genius may see an angelic choir. Looking *with* our eyes, the sun is only a blinding brilliance; looking *through* them as well, we see unplumbed mystery, the center of our wheeling solar system, the source of light and life. Looking again, we see our earth, offspring of the sun, and ourselves offspring, too. We see the first tender green shoot of the spring nudging through the matted leaves that fluttered down last fall, shoot and leaf both responding to the gentle, undeniable command of this yellow disk. There is hardly any limit here; this journey requires no fortune — only imagination. We think of the unique and delicate crystals of snow; we think of the seasons, and of all the strange cycles of birth and death, and life evolving toward consciousness and mind, toward laughter and love and deathless dreams. Truly the poet is not far from truth when seeing in his mind not a burning ball, but the multitude of the heavenly host, crying Holy, Holy, Holy.

"The sun, the moon, the stars, the seas, the hills, and the plains,—

Are not these, O soul, the vision of Him who reigns?
Is not the vision He, though He be not that which He seems?
Dreams are true while they last, and do we not live in dreams?
Earth, these solid stars, this weight of body and limb,
Are they not sign and symbol of thy division from Him?"

—ALFRED LORD TENNYSON (1809-92)

82   THE SUBLIME FAILURE

"And when he drew near and saw the city he wept over it, saying,
Would that even today you knew the things that make for peace!
But now they are hid from your eyes."

—LUKE 19:41-42

Strange behavior, this, for a man at the moment of his greatest worldly success, at the peak of his popularity, the summit of his fame. Riding upon an ass — symbolic of the peaceful nature of his mission — he approached the city and *wept* over it. Jesus was a failure, as men generally measure such things. Five short days would see him writhing on the tree, rejected as an imposter, executed as a disturber of the peace, betrayed by a disciple, denied by another, deserted by all. And the crowd that had lately cheered and waved their branches would stand by, silent, disillusioned.

Pilate was the success. He had power, prestige, wealth; and these three humbugs, as Lin Yutang calls them, have ever been the principal ingredients of success, popularly defined. Jesus neither had these things nor cared for them. "Possessions, outward success, publicity, luxury — to me these have always been contemptible," wrote Albert Einstein; "I believe that a simple, unassuming manner of life is best."

True success involves finding our real mission in life, and in following it faithfully and unswervingly. It means to serve God, whose names are Justice and Love and Truth, with our whole mind and heart. It means integrity, and loyalty to our highest vision. It means dipping down deep into our truest, strongest selves, to review our values, and then choosing those on which to stake our salvation. The cost of this, history demonstrates, may be great — martyrdom, perhaps, apparent failure all too probably.

"What shall it profit a man, if he shall gain the whole world, and lose his own soul?"

—MARK 8:36

Let me not fear poverty, let me fear self-betrayal. Let me not care for the plaudits of men, but for the approbation of my own conscience. Let me not seek power over the lives of others, but the conquest of myself. And, acquiescing in worldly failure, let me come at last to a true victory of the spirit.

83   BEHOLDEN

"It is more blessed to give than to receive; yet a noble nature can accept and be thankful."

—AUGUST STRINDBERG (1849-1912)

Every day of my life I live beholden to others.

I am beholden to those who have been guardians of man's heritage of knowledge and wisdom, stewards of the truths, beauties, and goodnesses which are our human legacy: my life is wondrously enhanced by those who have gone before.

I am beholden to all creative spirits — wordsmiths, smearers of pigment, chiselers of marble, midwives of music — all who have opened my eyes and ears to beauty; and to those thinkers of deep thoughts, who have looked beyond the known into the unknown: their creations and wisdom guide my way.

I am beholden to all those who have sought new truths, confident that new light will break forth to illumine man's way into the future; to scientists who have patiently probed into the hidden meanings of nature, finding order in its variety and law in its constancy: they have enabled me to live more comfortably and confidently upon the earth.

I am beholden to those who from my cradle have befriended me, whose kindnesses have renewed my hope, whose encouragement has restored my faith, whose love has taught me the meaning of love and enabled me to be more loving: they have made the world seem a friendlier place and given meaning to my days.

O my soul, seeing that I am so deeply in debt, shall I not give thanks for the richness of life and the goodness of being? Shall I not accept the days of my years with gladness, and endeavor to give back in return into the lives of others what is in my power to give, through kindness and cheerfulness, thoughtfulness and honesty, loyalty, bravery and honor?

"Be grateful to the man you help, think of him as God. Is it not a great privilege to be allowed to worship God by helping your fellow-man?"

—VIVEKANANDA (1863-1902)

84 REVERENCE BEFORE MISFORTUNE

"There is nothing more expressive of a barbarous and stupid lack of culture than the half-unconscious attitude so many of us slip into, of taking for granted, when we see weak, neurotic, helpless, drifting, unhappy people, that it is by reason of some especial favour towards us that the gods have given us an advantage over such persons."

—JOHN COWPER POWYS (1872-1963)

One of the inescapable facts of life is here suggested. We do not start equal. Perhaps we are fortunate in our ancestry, in our environment, or in our temperament. We have done nothing to deserve our parents — or a great many other blessings. Moreover, misfortune is not equally meted out. One man goes through unscathed; his neighbor is plagued at every turn. The proverb "misfortunes never come singly" points to the unfairness of the hands life deals.

Mr. Powys said that "it is all a matter of luck." We do not believe in luck; nor do we believe in a capricious God. But we agree with his conclusion: "The more culture we have, the more deeply do we resolve that in our relations to our world we shall feel nothing but plain, simple, humble reverence before the mystery of misfortune." Whoever thinks seriously upon the suffering and the injustice of the world will find any false sense of superiority oozing away. In the presence of all the cruelly handicapped, he will say: "This might be me; yes, and tomorrow it may be me."

The mystery of misfortune is inscrutable. We must not say: "God wills it." True, a world without suffering and struggle would be a world without joy and growth. But no God wills the idiot's birth, or any other form of irredeemable tragedy. One thing alone is clear: that is the part we are called upon to play. We are to feel "nothing but plain, simple, humble reverence before the mystery of misfortune." And feeling thus, we are to labor unremittingly to alleviate that suffering, heal these wounds. Whoever we are, we are called to the ministry of love.

> *"Solitude and hunger and weariness of spirit — these sharpened my perceptions so that I suffered not only my own sorrow but the sorrow of those about me. I was no longer myself. I was man. I was no longer a young girl . . . I was the oppressed. I was the drug addict, screaming and tossing in her cell, beating her head against the wall. I was that shoplifter who for rebellion was sentenced to solitary. I was that woman who had killed her children, murdered her lover."*

—DOROTHY DAY (1897-   )

85   NOT A TRANSACTION BUT A TRANSFORMATION

"The Mass should always be an action, and one that puts things together . . . But it is never a transaction. It is a transformation: of matter to meaning, crowd to community, bread to body, life to hope and (occasionally) dullness to delight."

—JOSEPH T. NOLAN (Contemporary)

How many have given up church-going, Protestant and Catholic, because all they have found on Sunday mornings was a transaction rather than a transformation? But how better can genuine worship be described: the finding of meaning, the alchemy transforming "crowd to community," "life to hope," and even, if rarely, "dullness to delight."

It is because such transformation is essential that we cannot outgrow the need to worship. We can abandon the all-too-human institution called the Church, or, better, we can labor to transform it, but the search for and discovery of meaning remains fundamental human business. The "lonely crowd" must somehow undergo metamorphosis into a beloved community, a fellowship of the concerned, a society that cares. Religious liberals have often spoken of "the commonplace of miracle." Rejecting the supposed miracle called "Transubstantiation," they have opted for a broader belief, that all life is utterly miraculous, that "every cubic inch of space is a miracle," as Whitman said, while a wee mouse is sufficient miracle to stagger "sextillions of infidels." But if all life is incredibly wonderful, and bread is forever being transformed to body and hence to spirit, we humans give little evidence of really

112

knowing it. Another poet writes: "Holy this earth, where unamazed we dwell." Alas, how true. And worship is the determined effort to strip the blindness from our eyes, the deafness from our ears, the hopelessness from our hearts. It is making way for those precious, rarer moments when dullness is transformed to delight, and "our cup runneth over."

"It is perseverence in the spiritual life, on and on, across the years and the changes of our moods and trials, health and environment: it is this that supremely matters."
—FRIEDRICH VON HUGEL (1852-1925)

86   TRUTH IN THE INWARD BEING

"Only they who carry sincerity to the highest point, in whom there remains not a single hair's breadth of hypocrisy, can see the hidden springs of things. The truly great man is he who does not lose his child-heart. He does not think beforehand that his words shall be sincere, nor that his actions shall be resolute; he simply always abides in the right."
—ANCIENT CHINESE

The words are old, but they speak directly to us. Sincerity is at the core of all real religion, for without it all other virtues become corrupted. Praise becomes flattery; love, pretense; honesty, "the best policy;" bravery, bravado; kindness, condescension.

We live in a world where pretense, like gold-mine stock, promises large dividends. A longtime best-seller tells us how "to win friends and influence people." All too much, "apple-polishing" is regarded as the quickest way "to get ahead." There is a crying need, in our world, for men who know that integrity — "truth in the inward being" — is a precious pearl to be guarded at whatever cost; men upon whom we can utterly depend to say what they mean and mean what they say, whose "yea is yea."

Our lives need careful, continuing, honest examination at this point. Do I carry sincerity to the highest point? Can it be said that no single hair's breadth of hypocrisy remains in me? Do I decry corruption in politics, and the general prevalence of crime, but lightly excuse what I would choose to regard as petty deceits and

113

"little white lies" and harmless subterfuges, as practiced by myself?

"Behold, thou desirest truth in the inward being; therefore teach me wisdom in my secret heart. Create in me a clean heart, O God, and put a new and right spirit within. Cast me not away from thy presence, and take not thy holy Spirit from me."

—PSALM 51: 6, 10, 11

87   SINS OF OMISSION

"I shall pass through this world but once. Any good therefore that I can do, or any kindness that I can show to any human being, let me do it now; let me not defer it or neglect it, for I may not pass this way again."

—ANONYMOUS

So often we miss opportunities to help others. We see the need, but irresolution delays us, and the chance passes; or, preoccupied with our own concerns, we fail to see. The ancient prayer speaks of "sins of omission" as well as of those of "commission." Committed sins are no doubt the more serious, but one suspects that numerically, at least, the sins of omission carry the day. Most people are not downright vicious; the evil in their nature is diluted. They are fairly respectable, reasonably good-natured and well-intentioned. They mean to be honest, fair, and kind. They are good, if not good for much.. It was of such that someone has written: all that is necessary for the victory of evil in this world is for the vast majority of good people to do nothing.

Any man had best seriously address himself to the question: Do I belong to that "vast majority" whose failure to act clears the way for wrong to prevail — for wars to continue, for rivers and oceans to be polluted, for racial discrimination to pollute our social life, for poverty to persist amid general plenty? Am I one of those who decry the world's ills, while doing nothing to banish them? Am I, like Saul at the stoning of Stephen, one of those who stands by silently consenting?

It may seem overly severe to say that those not actively opposing an evil state of affairs are as much to blame as those who are the primary perpetrators. An accomplice in a crime does at least something to help "pull it off." But is it not high time respectable

114

folk honestly faced up to the fact that passive goodness isn't enough? The individuals who really count are those who translate their good intentions into action, who carry through their resolution not to defer or neglect whatever good they can do, or kindness they can show. They are the ones who speak forthrightly when it would be easier to remain silent. They are the ones who call on the lonely shut-in, instead of just feeling sorry for him. They think: "This means me," instead of "Why doesn't somebody do something about it?" They say: "I am only one, but I am one. I cannot do everything, but I can do something. I cannot save the world single-handed, but what I can do I am not at liberty to omit."

"He who would do good to another, must do it in minute particulars. General good is the plea of the scoundrel, hypocrite, and flatterer."

—WILLIAM BLAKE (1757-1827)

88 MY FRIEND, MY ENEMY

"Your own self is your own Cain that murders your own Abel."
—WILLIAM LAW (1686-1761)

What an extraordinary insight. But man is a creature capable of occasional ecstacy and equally of despair; of undeniable heroism and of unspeakable degradation; a creature of insatiable desires and impossible hopes; torn by anxiety, made wretched by guilt, forever estranged yet forever seeking reconciliation; forever alone yet longing for warm, tender, meaningful relations with others; thirsting for righteousness yet driven as if by a devil inside him to destroy himself, his neighbor, his fairest creations.

With similar insight, the ancient Hindu scriptures tell us that "a man's own self is his friend; a man's own self is his foe." Strangely, we are both. And if we are truly to befriend ourselves, we shall have to learn in what ways we are our own worst enemy. An honest self-inventory reveals that we are more beast than angel. Our egocentricity is not easily routed, our callousness softened. Concupiscence is a word long out of fashion; but our nature is just as firmly concupiscent as in the olden days. We still experience the insatiability of human desires, the eternal dissatisfaction with what we have, the satanic attraction of what we have not and have no right to.

"I long ago decided," wrote David Grayson, in *The Friendly Road,* "to try to be fully what I am, and not to be anything or anybody else." Of course, we quickly agree. To be oneself constitutes a basic and primary purpose in living. Yet we know how easy it is for many people to live their entire lives without ever knowing how to belong to themselves. For if my own self is not only my friend but also my enemy, to be fully what I am involves accepting my own divided nature. Freud and Jung had serious differences, but they agreed in teaching many stark, uncomplimentary truths about human nature. They helped us become more realistic about the demonic forces buried within ourselves. Jesus taught men to love their enemies, and this means, Jung insisted, that we first of all learn to love the enemy in our own hearts. Hell may be a mythical place, but it is certainly a psychological reality. Man is a creature all too prone to sabotage his own life. Within us all there is a tug-of-war between the wish for life and the wish for death. And while relatively few people actually take their own life by an act of direct violence, many commit suicide gradually, by alchoholism, by over-work, by inviting accidents, by inducing illness. Sir Thomas Browne spoke of this, in his classic sentence: "There's another man inside me who is angry at me."

Self-acceptance, then, means looking as deeply into our own hearts as we can; looking honestly, fearlessly, neither condemning nor condoning what we find there, but rather using it as the basis for transforming ourselves, as Father Yelchaninov put it, "into the image and likeness of God." The proper goal is not just trying to be "fully what I am." It is using self-knowledge as the basis for growing more fully human and compassionate, courageous and free. Acceptance of what we are, and the determination to be our self, at whatever cost, is the first essential step toward a greater goal in life: the becoming what we are capable of becoming.

"If I am not for myself, who will be for me?"
—THE TALMUD (c. 375 A.D.)

". . . he hath left you all his walks,
His private arbors and new-planted orchards,
On this side of Tiber; he hath left them you,
And to your heirs forever; common pleasures,
To walk abroad and recreate yourselves."
        (Marc Antony, of Julius Caesar, to the citizens of Rome)
          —WILLIAM SHAKESPEARE (1564-1616)

Though many people nowadays suffer from what Philip Wylie has called "motorosis" — a disease whose chief symptom is never walking anywhere you can ride — man is by nature a pedestrian. Walking is his natural means of locomotion, and is something he needs to do, just like eating, sleeping, and breathing. His muscles need stretching and contracting, his lungs fresh air. Both brain and stomach work better for the man who walks, who likes to walk, and sees to it that no day passes without a walk. Doctors from Hippocrates to Paul Dudley White, and no doubt your own physician, have regularly recommended walking, to improve the circulation of the blood, aid digestion, reduce weight, calm the nerves, and cure insomnia. Trevelyan, an inveterate hiker, used to say he had two doctors, his left leg and his right. Christopher Morley called walking "a never-failing remedy for the blues."

Psycho-somatic medicine reminds us that many of the ills our bodies fall heir to are emotionally induced. Our psychic disturbances, our unhappiness, anxiety, and unacknowledged fears can all produce physical symptoms. With our present-day emphasis on psychology, we are apt to overlook the opposite side of the coin: the body also affects our state of mind. Physical unfitness is apt to induce poor spirits, while well-conditioned muscles, good circulation, plenty of oxygen sucked into the lungs generally produce a lifting of the spirit, a calming of the nerves, a sense of joy and well-being.

Juvenal's "a sound mind in a sound body" is still sound advice. Body and mind in harmony, this is a secret of health. As every chronic invalid knows only too well, maintaining a cheerful disposition and healthy outlook despite bodily weariness and stringent limitations, to say nothing of recurring pain, is an heroic task.

Walking is as much a spiritual exercise as a physical one. If we go alone, we can think, indeed are bound to think. Many find swinging along at a comfortable gait especially provocative of thought. Poets have often found it the best way to write their poems, or at least get them launched; and scientific researchers have sometimes had long-sought solutions to knotty problems literally burst into their consciousness, as they strode along. Anyone is apt to find walking a good way to work on his problems and set his thoughts in order. And he who is a nature-lover and has accesss to open country is twice blest. Many will agree with John Burroughs, the naturalist, who liked best to walk with his dog. "A dog," he wrote, "is a true pedestrian. He is constantly sniffing adventure, laps at every spring, looks upon every field and wood as a new world to be explored." If we have lost the art of walking, perhaps our dogs can re-teach us.

"A walk: the air incredibly pure, delights for the eye, a warm and gently caressing sunlight, one's whole being joyous . . . The whole country seemed to me like a censer, and the morning was a prayer. It is good to meditate here, to live, dream and die."

—HENRI FRÉDÉRIC AMIEL (1821-81)

90 A MAN AND NOT A GOD

"Jesus was a man and not a god, and therein lies our wonder and our surprise."

—KAHLIL GIBRAN (1883-1931)

In early Christian days, many would have reversed this statement. They did not doubt that Jesus was God, but questioned his manhood. Had not his appearance on earth been just that — an appearance, an apparition? This was the heresy known as Docetism, and it was vigorously fought by the early Church, which has ever since maintained he was both "very God of very God" and truly man, "flesh of our flesh." Today, our "heresy" is that of the Syrian poet; we agree with him. To deify Jesus, to see in him a unique supernatural significance, lessens his significance for us. It is his humanity that causes our wonder and surprise. This is what human life can be like. Such are the possibilities which lie latent in us. Perhaps we cannot be such men as he; humility makes us shrink

118

from the idea. He was a genius, and therefore, in a sense, inimitable. We are not geniuses; no matter how hard we try, we cannot equal the brilliance of Einstein, or write plays as great as Shakespeare's. But "we are," as a wise ancient put it, "as holy as we *will* to be." And the import of Jesus' message, we think, is that men are capable of divine sonship, here and now. The kingdom of heaven is at hand, not to be ushered in by some radical social revolution, but just by you and me discovering who we really are, and acting accordingly.

So, as we contemplate the significance to ourselves and our race of the life and martyrdom of Jesus, we particularly cherish the intimations which the Gospels give us of his humanity. It is not Jesus, the divine hero, calmly enacting a supernatural role, that appeals to us. Our wonder grows as we see him in all his human frailty — weary, discouraged, lonely; as we read of his being "sorrowful and sore troubled," or his saying to Peter: "What, could ye not watch with me one hour?" It surely was not man's natural fear of death that caused his agony in the Garden of Gethsemane; it was his uncertainty what God's will for him really was. Here was a brave man, an utterly dedicated man, facing "life's central test." And his prayer, while sublime, was also very human: "Father, if it be possible, let this cup pass away from me: Nevertheless, not as I will, but as thou wilt." Therefore our wonder grows, and our loyalty is captured.

We give thanks for the magnificent humanity of Jesus, our brother and our friend, and for the vision of the possibilities of life embodied in all christlike lives; may that vision inspire us and, like some clarion, call us forth from our camp of ease to new battles of the spirit.

91   OPEN-EYED, OPEN-HANDED

"Have I knowledge? confounded it shrivels
  at Wisdom laid bare.
Have I forethought? how purblind, how blank,
  to the Infinite Care!
Do I task any faculty highest, to image success?

119

I but open my eyes, — and perfection, no more
and no less,
In the kind I imagined, full-fronts me, and
God is seen God
In the star, in the stone, in the flesh,
in the soul and the clod."

—ROBERT BROWNING (1812-89)

Let me be open-eyed: observant of the perpetual miracle of life and love on this fragment of a star flung across the infinity of space; appreciative of earth's symphony of color, harmony of shape, and ubiquity of beauty; alert to the wonderfulness of little children, the strength and dignity in ordinary men and women, the unsung heroism — to all the sublimities, all the gratifying nuances of the human story, to every intimation of divinity in the lives around me.

Let me be open-eared: tuned in to all the varied music of the world: to man-made melodies, and to the songs of wind and water, insect and bird. Let me be responsive to the call to adventure, the summons to high endeavor, the appeal to conscience; and to the "still, sad music of humanity" — the falling of human tears, the anguish wrenched from human hearts.

Let me be open-minded: receptive to unfamiliar thoughts, to strange viewpoints, and brand-new ideas, making doubly certain to give fair hearing to all that challenges my complacency, my prejudgments, my unexamined assumptions.

Let me be open-handed: ready to share earth's bounty, to meet my fellowman, stranger as well as neighbor, with trust, expecting to find him where he ought to be. Let me eschew all miserly clutching, all grasping at life as though it were not more blessed to give than to receive.

Let me open my mouth: not in foolish boast or much speaking, but to utter the word of courage, the word of cheer, the word of sympathy and hope. Let me sing with the Psalmist: "Lord, open thou my lips; and my mouth shall show forth thy praise."

BLESSED ARE THEY THAT REMEMBER

"Our lives take their meaning from their interlacing with other lives, and when one life is ended those into which it was woven are also carried into darkness. Neither you nor I, but only the hand of time, slow-moving, yet sure and steady, can lift that blanket of blackness."

—ADLAI STEVENSON (1900-65)

If, as the philosophers tell us, we have no true wealth save what we carry within us, our minds should be our treasure house. A mind well-stocked with happy memories is the truest kind of wealth.

One of time's greatest boons is its softening of the angularities of pain. Sorrow's wounds heal, though not without scar. Grief's sharp jabbing thrusts or its aching emptiness give way to peace and sanctifying memory. That which has been, and is no more, remains within the mind to bless. The anguish is drained away. Remembering, we discover the meaning of the beatitude: "Blessed are they that mourn, for they shall be comforted." "To suffer passes away," say the French; "but to have suffered never passes."

According to an ancient legend, a woman came to the river Styx, to be ferried to the land of departed spirits. Charon, the ferryman, reminded her of her privilege to drink of the waters of Lethe, which grant forgetfulness of the life she was leaving. "I will forget how I have suffered," she exclaimed. "Yes," replied Charon, "and also how you have rejoiced." "I will forget how I have been hated." "And also," said the kindly ferryman, "how you have been loved." After thinking it over, the woman left the draught of Lethe untasted. Better the mingled memories of suffering and sorrow, joy and love, than oblivion.

Our ancestors offered prayers for the dead. We do not believe they need our prayers to help them through purgatory. But it is good that we should not forget those we "have loved and lost awhile." We need some other way to keep their memory fresh. How better than when, while quiet and alone, we let one and another face come to mind, called up from some mysterious mental treasure room. Perhaps it is our mother's face; and we think of what she has meant to us — what she taught, what she saw in us and hoped for us. Or perhaps it is a wise teacher of our childhood, or a beloved companion of former years. Golden memories come flooding in, bringing healing and cleansing. Sometimes they awaken old resolves, or point to present opportunities. They teach us our true priorities, help us to see how right the poet was who said that the little unremembered acts of kindness constitute the best part of a man's life.

"Many waters cannot quench love, neither can the floods drown it."

—SONG OF SOLOMON, 8:7

93   A THING MOST NECESSARY

"To keep a few friends, but these without capitulation — above all, on the same grim condition, to keep friends with himself — here is a task for all that a man has of fortitude and delicacy."
—ROBERT LOUIS STEVENSON (1850-94)

In this day when sexual love and romance hold the spotlight, it seems important to remind ourselves that friendship is in some ways the highest form of love, the least selfish and often the most enduring. Unlike matrimony, it is not fed by sexual attraction and passion, nor maintained by family responsibilities and the presence of children; nor is it maintained by a legal contract and by vows solemnly undertaken. One can understand, even if one disagrees, why some have argued that married love is impossible, because contractual. Freedom is, at least, an indispensable condition of friendship.

So, when Gibran, in *The Prophet,* wrote: "Love one another, but make not a bond of love," he was not really talking about marriage, but about friendship. Of course, mates can be friends. Would that they always were. But marriage is bonded love; friendship, pure and simple, requires no relinquishment of personal freedom.

Like "love," "friendship" is a word too loosely and broadly used. Letters from strangers begin "Dear Friend." And "he's a friend of mine" is apt only to mean "an acquaintance." One would like to see the word reserved for those intimate few with whom we share our lives in meaningful ways, whose interests and tastes we share, with whom little needs to be held back or concealed. As William Penn once wrote: "A true friend unbosoms freely, advises justly, assists readily, adventures boldly, takes all patiently, defends courageously, and continues a friend unchangeably."

So defined, how many friendships can one afford? Friendly relations with many acquaintances, yes, of course. But true friends to whom one "unbosoms freely" must be chosen carefully. He is fortunate who has even one. For such friendship is the one sure antidote for loneliness, a virtual guarantee of happiness in the midst of life's trials and tribulations.

We do not always understand that real friendship involves equality. Perhaps occasionally it can develop between parent and child, teacher and pupil, rich man and poor. Kinship can become friendship. Yet Samuel Johnson shrewdly observed that friendship is seldom lasting except between equals: "Benefits which cannot be repaid and obligations which cannot be discharged are not commonly found to increase affection."

"Friendship is a thing most necessary to life, since without friends no one would choose to live, though possessed of all other advantages."

—ARISTOTLE (384-322 B.C.)

94 WHEN SO MUCH HAS BEEN GIVEN

"Prayer is only another name for good, clean, direct thinking. When you pray, think well what you are saying, and make your thoughts into things that are solid. In that manner, your prayer will have strength, and that strength shall become part of you, mind, body and spirit."

—RICHARD LLEWELLYN (1907-   )

To what wealth do we fall heir, we humans; of what extraordinary bounty are we, all too frequently, the ungrateful recipients. When so much has been given — clean air to breathe, sunshine, moisture, nourishing soil, beauty, a rich and varied human heritage, and good companions for our passage — how should we pray? Not, surely, as petitioners pleading for special favors from a magician god. Let ours be a prayer for clear, clean, honest thinking; a genuine repentance; a firm resolve to live courageously, to love life, always trying to meet it halfway. Let ours be a prayer of deeds as well as words, a prayer for awareness of man's injustice and blindness and sin — an injustice we too easily overlook, a blindness we so generally share, a sin to which we are not stranger.

Where justice is denied, let our response be anger. Where old wrongs go unrighted and poverty's vicious circle shrinks life to hopelessness, let us know concern. Where ignorance constricts, let us not be callous. Whatever diminishes the lives of others, we would not forget diminishes our own; for we are involved in mankind. We share man's triumphs and achievements, but we are robbed where his potentialities go unrealized. Where there is darkness in the lives of others, our own vision of the world is dimmed. Where men are sick in body or in spirit, our own health is undermined.

Where there is wrong, we would summon clear-headed courage to fight it. Where there is social evil, we pray for determination to wrestle against it. And where there is joy and laughter and love, let us share it gladly and enlarge it. So may we give thanks by helping in ways however small to make our world a fit habitation for all the sons of men. So may the ancient prayer at last be fulfilled that God's will be done on earth.

"May no hatred against us enter the heart of any man nor hatred of any man enter our heart;

May no envy of us enter the heart of any man nor envy of any man enter our heart.

May thy Torah be our occupation all the days of our life."

—THE TALMUD (c. 375 A.D.)

95 A TRULY HUMAN EXISTENCE

"What we need to realize is that whatever small decency we have in our hearts is just as magnificently capacitated by science and technology as is our willingness to murder."

—GERARD PIEL (1915-   )

This is indeed something we do need to keep reminding ourselves. The problems threatening man's future are legion, noisy, and alarming. No thinking person should seek to minimize the seriousness of our human situation. Yet it is also true that at last man has the ability to eliminate poverty, to minimize pain, to bring the food supply and population into balance. We can, if we will, eliminate war, and put our genius for invention at the service of mankind's well-being.

To say we can doesn't mean that we will. The odds are against it. But unless we do believe that we can, it is certain that we won't. So let us keep as clearly as we can before us the picture of a truly human existence.

A truly human existence involves more than a mass of standardized conveniences, a multiplicity of possessions, more than an adequate diet and good medical care from cradle to grave. The physical basis for life is important. But once provided, factors of deeper importance assume priority. We discover that what gives life meaning, savor, and dignity are moral and spiritual values; beauty, brotherhood, and creativity — all that fosters the realization of man's capacity to go beyond himself, to transcend the purely physical limits of his existence. To be subjugated by things is for men as much an assault on their dignity as to be subjugated by their fellows.

We stand on the threshold, now, of the time when neither producing food, nor manufacture and distribution of material goods need to be the principal ends for which men must labor. With the energy of the universe at their disposal, men can focus their major attention on the creation of that which machines cannot produce — human services of all kinds, artistry, handcraft of all sorts, and education, not as factual learning so much as encouragement along the road to personal fulfillment. The expectation that men grow happier and become better by being taught to read, to develop their rational capacities, and improve their material status we now know to have been naive. But we can make education aim at helping us achieve a truly human existence. It can help us learn how to transform idleness, time that is empty and impersonal and must be wiled away, into leisure, which is time we are free to invest in ourselves, "the most precious time of all."

We can, if we will.

"Dark and cold we may be, but this
Is no winter now. The frozen misery
Of centuries breaks, cracks, begins to move;
The thunder is the thunder of the floes,

The thaw, the flood, the upstart spring.
Thank God our time is now when wrong
Comes up to face us everywhere,
Never to leave us till we take
The longest stride of soul men ever took."

—CHRISTOPHER FRY (1907-   )

96   CONSCIOUSNESS OF SANCTITY IN EXISTENCE

"The religion of the future must have as its basis the consciousness of sanctity in existence — in common things, in events of human life, in the gradually comprehended, interlocking whole revealed to the human desire for knowledge, in the benedictions of beauty and love, in the catharsis, the sacred purging, of the moral drama in which character is pitted against fate and even the deepest tragedy may uplift the mind."

—JULIAN HUXLEY (1887-   )

Let me recognize divinity in the world in all its varied manifestations and disguises: in the mysterious depths of my own being; in the call to spiritual adventure, urging me on to better ends; in the daily witness of nature's unfailing order and providence; in the countless quiet heroisms of ordinary persons. Let me not fail to see intimations of divinity even in the unlikeliest places. Let me attend, perceive, and cherish the persistent testimony that despite all man-caused dislocations and disenchantments, the heart of reality is sound.

Let me link my life to all such manifestations and intimations. Let me also link my life in ever-stronger bonds to my fellowmen, continuing to grow in love, coming nearer to friend and stranger in understanding of our mutual weaknesses and strengths, cultivating empathy, and persistently seeking true meeting and genuine concern.

Let me bow in shame in acknowledgment of my share of guilt in my nation's failure to pursue the roads to peace, and to do the things that make for peace. I have been silent when I should have spoken out; by my silence I have consented to what I know is wrong. I have not done enough to help secure justice and fair play for those still denied their basic human rights. May my intention to seek understanding, my refusal to judge and condemn, my determination to create peace and pursue it be kindled into a fire that will help to melt the walls of suspicion and hate that fragment the world and impoverish brotherhood.

Let me not forget all those who stand in need of comfort and courage; those who suffer in body and in spirit; those waiting the release of death; all children who go hungry and malnourished for want of food, for want of love; for all men everywhere in whatsoever kind of bondage and exile, spiritual no less than physical. Let me not forget the never-ending struggle of my race, all its agony, confusion, and heartbreak. Neither let me be paralyzed by its magnitude nor driven to despair. With compassion ever renewed, let me take up ministry to my neighbor in need, and whatever it is possible for me to do, do promptly and cheerfully.

And let me believe, O let me believe that out of pain and suffering mankind may yet learn what it must learn, if man is to endure, and to prevail.

"This is a world in which each of us, knowing his limitations, knowing the evils of superficiality and the terrors of fatigue, will have to cling to what is close to him, to what he knows, to what he can do, to his friends and his tradition and his love, lest he be dissolved in a universal confusion and know nothing and love nothing . . .

"This cannot be an easy life. We shall have a rugged time of it to keep our minds open and to keep them deep, to keep our sense of beauty and our ability to make it, and our occasional ability to see it in places remote and strange and unfamiliar; we shall have a rugged time of it, all of us, in keeping these gardens in our villages, in keeping open the manifold, intricate, casual paths, to keep these flourishing in a great, open, windy world; but this, as I see it, is the condition of man; and in this condition we can help, because we can love, one another."

—J. ROBERT OPPENHEIMER (1904-   )

"And the Voice went forth throughout the world . . . and each one heard it according to his capacity; old men and youths and boys and sucklings and women: the Voice was to each one as each one had the power to receive it."

—SHEMOTH

A Moslem legend tells how Moses once overheard a shepherd praying: "O God, show me where thou art, that I may become thy servant. I will clean thy shoes, and comb thy hair, and sew thy clothes, and fetch thee milk." Moses angrily rebuked him: "God is a Spirit, and needs not such gross ministrations." The shepherd, dismayed and ashamed, fled to the desert, there to be met by ministering angels; but Moses heard a voice: "O Moses, wherefore have you driven away my servant? I regard not the words that are spoken, but the heart that offers them."

We cannot conceive of God except in terms that we know. We know better than the crude anthropomorphism of the shepherd. In whatever sense it may be that man is made in God's image, we can be confident that God is not made in our image. Yet every man can only worship according to his capacity, his understanding. Simple, sincere devotion is preferable to spiritual arrogance or a coldly critical attitude. To think of God too humanly would seem a less grievous error than to think of him abstractly and impersonally. God is not "a person." He is not less than "a person" — but infinitely more.

Without belittling the philosopher's endeavor to comprehend the incomprehensible, to define the indefinable, let it be said that the more important effort is to be aware of that power which is within us, yet infinitely beyond us — to be aware of it, attentive to it, obedient to it. The great need is a deeper consciousness of the creative life which we share. It is to know that our little love is part of a big Love, our spirits are linked to infinite spirit. It is to allow ourselves to be drawn toward excellence, toward unending increase of life. It is to follow that persistent summons, that upward urge, that "potent, felt, interior command." If we harken to this "voice," however we individually hear it, our definitions of God cease to be of primary importance.

"Truly it is life that shines forth in all things! Vast, heavenly, of unthinkable form, it shines forth . . . It is farther than the far, yet near at hand, set down in the secret place of the heart . . . Not by sight is it grasped, not even by speech, but by the peace of knowledge, one's nature purified — in that way, by meditating, one does behold him who is without form."

—THE UPANISHADS (800-600 B.C.)

98   TRUTH OR REPOSE

"God offers to every mind its choice between truth and repose. Take which you please — you can never have both. He in whom the love of repose predominates will accept the first creed, the first philosophy, the first political party he meets — most likely his father's. He gets rest, commodity and reputation; but shuts the door of truth. He in whom love of truth predominates will keep himself aloof from all moorings, and afloat. He submits to the inconvenience of suspense and imperfect opinion, but is a candidate for truth, as the other is not, and respects the highest law of his being."

—RALPH WALDO EMERSON (1803-82)

The willingness to choose truth above repose makes one a religious liberal. Readiness to doubt and the keeping of one's mind ajar may not conduce to comfort, but they prevent stagnation and are required of those who would be loyal truth-seekers.

"Sit down before fact as a little child," wrote Thomas Huxley to Charles Kingsley; "be prepared to give up every preconceived notion, follow humbly wherever and to whatever abysses nature leads, or you shall learn nothing." It is the facts not only about nature and the universe, but also about ourselves that need so to be faced if we would learn truth. Perhaps our preconceived notions about ourselves are the hardest to give up. Our self-portrait is quite different from our image in the mirror of truthfulness.

Nevertheless, one wonders if there is, or need be, quite so irreconcilable a choice between truth and repose as Emerson suggests. Does not the man who has resolved to be "a candidate for truth" win a new kind of repose? So Huxley testified in the same letter: "I have only begun to learn content and peace of mind since

129

I have resolved at all risks to do this."

"It is necessary to the happiness of man that he be mentally faithful to himself. Infidelity does not consist in believing or disbelieving; it consists in professing to believe what he does not believe. It is impossible to calculate the moral mischief that mental lying has produced in society."

—THOMAS PAINE (1737-1809)

99   THOU LIFE THAT FILLEST ALL

"If the doors of perception were cleansed, everything would appear as it is — infinite. For man has closed himself up, till he sees all things through the narrow chinks of his cavern."

—WILLIAM BLAKE (1757-1827)

To that nameless Spirit, too great to be known, too wonderful to be taken for granted, too mysterious to be understood, I now address my thoughts — the longings, needs, doubts, hopes that are my prayer:

Art thou not nearer than we know, nearer than we are to ourselves, nearer to us, as the Sufi poet said, then we to our own jugular vein? Men look for thee in far places, searching for miracles to startle them; yet is not every person a walking, breathing, thinking miracle? Men skim the surface in vain pursuit, unaware of what lies quietly in the depths of their own being.

Dost thou hide from me, thou ubiquitous holiness? Or am I fugitive from thee? I have cluttered my life with possessions, and busied my mind with trivia. Art thou truly silent, or is my spirit too restless, my thoughts too noisy for me to hear thy word for me? Now let me take another path — simplify my life, empty my mind, until enlightenment like the rising sun drives away the mist and shadows of night. Let me turn away from the confusion of much speaking, and all tangential activities, to possess myself, so that without distraction I may wait upon thee with quiet expectation.

If thou art to be found in all things, then let me find thee in the people with whom I live and work and play. Let me reach out in empathy and compassion to all those, known to me and unknown, whom life threatens to overwhelm, whom circumstances imprison, whom poverty crushes into hopelessness and apathy. Let me not forget that everyone has an oubliette hidden within him that holds him prisoner. Let me discover tangible and immediate ways of alleviating some small part of the world's oceanic misery. Let me be an answer to somebody's prayer, a helping hand, a perceptive listener, a loving presence. By my cheerfulness, my kindness and acceptance, may I help someone else this day to self-respect, to renewed courage and hope.

So may I go from today into each tomorrow as one determined to be himself, and to be a doer of the works of righteousness and truth and not a hearer only. I would live as one stubbornly seeking fully to be before he dies, as one fully awakened to his true estate as a shareholder in the spiritual magnificence which is revealed to man in his finest, truest moments of insight.

"May I be born again and again, and suffer thousands of miseries, so that I may worship the only God that exists, the only God I believe in, the sum of all souls — and, above all, my God the wicked, my God the miserable, my God the poor of all races, of all species."

—VIVEKANANDA (1863-1902)

100   IF NOT NOW, WHEN?

"It is eternity now. I am in the midst of it. It is about me in the sunshine."

—RICHARD JEFFERIES (1848-97)

Martin Buber had a saying I like, really an epigram: "If not now, when?" Life slips by so easily. Not only our neighbors to the South, we all say "mañana, mañana." We put off. We fail to speak out. We let time flow, as though we had forever. But we have only this moment. About so much we need to inquire, Buber-wise: "If not now, when?"

It is not the fact of death that makes life tragic so much as that many of us allow death to creep into us before we die — death in the form of hardening of the mental arteries: the betrayal of our

131

gifts, the death of integrity, of creativity, and that awareness which opens a man to the pain and glory of life.

"Let the dead bury their dead," said Jesus. It was a harsh statement. Did he mean: There in the city, and about you in the countryside are the living dead, but, my disciples, do not join them, do not allow them to entomb you?

Put positively, heaven is not a future state but a matter of present awareness. Do not ask to go on living after the death of your body. Live now, squeezing the apple of all its juice! Should there be a life beyond this life, though we can hardly wish for one or imagine it, how better to prepare for it? If not, we can gladly affirm the goodness of this day and the value of this life.

"It may be that we cease; we cannot tell.
Even if we cease, life is a miracle."

—JOHN MASEFIELD (1878-1967)

ACKNOWLEDGMENTS

For permission to use quotations from copyright material in this volume, grateful acknowledgment is made to the following authors, translators, agents, and publishers:

George Allen & Unwin Ltd. for quotations from *Three Ways of Thought in Ancient China*, 1939, by Arthur Waley; and *Christianity and the Religions of the World*, 1939, by Albert Schweitzer, translated by Johanna Powers.

Cambridge University Press for the passage from *Mamre*, by Martin Buber; and with Macmillan Publishing Co. for the passage from *Religion in the Making*, by Alfred North Whitehead.

Columbia University Press for the passage from *Man's Right to Knowledge* (2nd Series), New York: Herbert Muschel, 1954, by J. Robert Oppenheimer, "Prospects in the Arts and Sciences," by permission of the Trustees of Columbia University in the city of New York.

The John Day Co. and Thomas Y. Crowell Co., Inc., for the passage from *The Way of Life According to LaoTzu*, translated by Witter Bynner, 1944.

Doubleday and Co., and Dr. Margaret Mead, for the quotation from her book, *Culture and Commitment*, 1970.

E. P. Dutton & Co., Inc., for the quotation from the *The Story of San Michele* by Axel Munthe, 1929; renewal © 1951 by Major Malcolm Munthe; and for the passage from *Across the Unknown* by Stewart Edward White, Copyright, 1939 by E. P. Dutton & Co.; renewal © 1967 by R. E. Bixby.

Paul Engle for his quatrain from "Letter to an Older Generation," from his volume of poems, *American Song*, 1934.

Harcourt Brace Jovanovich, Inc., for two passages from *Modern Man in Search of a Soul*, by Carl Gustav Jung.

Harper & Row for quotations from *A Testament of Devotion*, by Thomas R. Kelly, 1941; *The Ordeal of Change*, by Eric Hoffer, 1964; *The Long Loneliness*, by Dorothy Day, 1952; and with A. D. Peters & Co., Ltd., London, for the passage from *Religion Without Revelation*, by Julian Huxley, Revised Edition, 1957.

Alfred A. Knopf for the quotations from *The Spirit of Liberty: Papers and Addresses of Learned Hand*, edited by Irving Dilliard, 1952; and *Science in the Cause of Man*, 1961, by Gerard Piel.

Macmillan Publishing Co., New York, and Macmillan Press, Hampshire, England, for the quotation from *Sadhana*, by Rabindranath Tagore. To Macmillan Publishing Co. for the quotation from *How Green Was My Valley*, by Richard Llewellyn, 1939. To Macmillan Publishing Co. and The Society of Authors, London, as the literary representative of the Estate of John Masefield for the couplet by John Masefield, from his *Sonnets and Other Poems*, 1916.

The National Catholic Reporter for a quotation from the article, "Three Masses that Changed Me," by Joseph T. Nolan, Nov. 20, 1970.

W. W. Norton & Co., Inc., for two quotations from *The Meaning of Culture*, by John Cowper Powys.

Oxford University Press for the lines from *The Sleep of Prisoners*, by Christopher Fry.

Princeton University Press for the quotation from TWO ADDRESSES, by St. John Perse, Bollingen Series LXXXVI, *On Poetry*, translated by W. H. Auden, © 1961 by Bollingen Foundation.

Random House, Inc., for quotations from Dante's *Divine Comedy*, translated by Carlyle and Wicksteed, 1932; and *Fires of Spring*, by James A. Michener, 1949.

Charles Scribners' Sons for quotations from *Marlborough, His Life and Times*, by Winston S. Churchill; and *Soliloquies in England*, by George Santayana, 1922.

Schocken Books Inc. for the quotation from *Tales of the Hasidim: The Early Masters*, by Martin Buber, Copyright © 1947 by Schocken Books Inc., Copyright renewed © 1975 by Schocken Books Inc.

Adlai E. Stevenson III for the quotation from his father's address at Phillip Murray's Memorial Service.

Charles E. Tuttle Co., Inc., for the haiku translated by Harold Stewart, in his *A Net of Fireflies*, 1960.

The University of Chicago Press for the quotation from *The Future of Mankind*, by Karl Jaspers, translated by E. B. Ashton, 1961.

Westminster Press for the quotation from *Honest to God*, by John A. T. Robinson, © SCM Press Ltd. 1963. Used by permission.

Yale University Press for the quotation from *The Meaning of God in Human Experience* by William E. Hocking.

Careful effort has been made to trace the ownership of all copyright material quoted. If any copyrights have been inadvertently infringed upon, the author offers his apologies and will be pleased to make proper acknowledgment in any future printing.

Grateful acknowledgment is also made to Essex Publishing Co. of Essex Junction, Vermont, which published the first edition of this book for Unity Church of Saint Paul, Minnesota, in 1972.